A PILGRIM'S GUIDE TO PRAYER

D0104412

Edward C. Briggs

BROADMAN PRESS
Nashville, Tennessee

Unless otherwise indicated, Scripture quotations are the author's translation. Scripture quotations marked (RSV) are from the Revised Standard Version of the Bible, copyrighted 1946, 1952, © 1971, 1973 by the National Council of the Churches of Christ in the U.S.A., and used by permission. Those marked (KJV) are from the King James Version of the Bible.

Dewey Decimal Classification: 248.3
Subject Heading: PRAYER
Library of Congress Catalog Card Number: 86-24410
Printed in the United States of America

Library of Congress Cataloging-in-Publication Data

Briggs, Edward C.
  A pilgrim's guide to prayer.

  1. Lord's prayer. 2. Prayer. 3. Prayers. I. Title.
BV230.B69 1987   248.3'2   86-24410
ISBN 0-8054-8156-7

To my father
Dr. David H. Briggs,
from whom I often learned
and with whom I sometimes suffered,
though at the time
not always knowing which.

PREFACE

There may be a lot of praying among Christians today, but there's a lot of not-praying, too. And half-praying. And proxy-praying, which is people letting others do it for us while we just listen. We have a need here, perhaps even a crisis of sorts.

When the money supply is strained, economists speak of a money crisis. If there isn't enough rain, we call it a drought. And a shortage of prayer leads just as surely to a spiritual crisis, for one person, or a church, or a family, or a nation.

The Bible says we (persons, churches, families, nations) "have not because we ask not." So, not praying means not having the things prayer obtains, such as love and joy and peace, the ties that bind our hearts, the forgiveness of sin, God's guidance in our lives.

James told us if we know good and don't do it it's sin. Which means not praying is a sin. Not just a problem, a *sin*.

Once in Israel's history, people demanded a king like other nations had. Samuel had his doubts but bowed to pressure and anointed Saul. At the same time, he gave warnings about the future if people put a king in the place of God. And the people said "Well, you pray for us, then." And Samuel said he would. He said, "Far be it from me that I should sin against the Lord by ceasing to pray for you." He went on urging them to fear the Lord and to serve Him with all their hearts. Or, as he put it, "You shall be swept away, both you and your king" (see 1 Sam. 12:19-24).

Far be it from me that I should sin against the Lord by ceasing to pray . . .

There we see how serious is not praying. And, by contrast, how valuable it is when we do.

Who can tell the worth of a prayer like this?

> O Lord, support us all the day long, until the shadows lengthen and the evening comes, and the busy world is hushed, and the fever of life is over, and our work is done. Then in thy mercy grant us a safe lodging, and a holy rest, and peace at last. Amen.

Prayer calls up the great questions of our existence. Is there a god? Is God this god? Is He involved with our world? Does He know and care about us? Can He help our situation? Will He?

Real prayer is like wrestling. It's a struggle, a sort of work. It's Jacob beside the Jabbok as a desperate dawn begins to break. It's Christ in Gethsemane. It's Paul in Romans 7 bemoaning the hold of sin on his life. It's Moses saying, "Blot me out of your Book, O Lord, if I can't save this nation" (Ex. 32:32).

Prayer is for souls what food is for bodies, gasoline for cars, money for retirements, film for cameras. In other words, it makes life work, and without it things grind to a halt.

Prayer isn't tame. Anything that's tame or loose or half-hearted can't be called prayer. Prayer sweats, crys, and gripes. It shouts, but never yawns. Nothing that yawns can be called a prayer. That strange and wonderful Baptist, John Bunyan, had it right. He said, "When thou prayest, rather let thy heart be without words, than thy words without heart!"

How serious is not praying? Well, how serious is not eating? Or not breathing? How serious is living life and never loving? How serious is not speaking to the best friend you ever had? How serious is being the branch of a vine and getting cut off?

Prayer is either the most practical and sensible of all human acts, or the most wasteful and ridiculous. It's one or the other but can't be both. And the important thing isn't what we *say* it is but how we *live like it is.*

Somewhere in Kentucky in the winter of 1816, missionary Luther Rice wrote in his journal, *Dispensations of Providence:*

> Mrs. P gives me an interesting account of the manner of life of her brother-in-law, John Quincy Adams—that he is a very pious man—always reads a chapter in the bible just before going to bed, & immediately on rising—retires at eleven, & rises at 4 o'clock, regularly—& loses no time during the day—keeps a journal of every occurrence—marks particularly his own advancement in either piety or knowledge—at the close of each month sets down a number of appropriate reflexions—In hearing this account of that great man, I felt convinced of a criminal waste of time, & indolence of habit in relation to real improvement, both in religion & knowledge, which I hope I may have grace in some degree hereafter to correct.

This is from a man who was extremely disciplined in his own spiritual life. So when you read it you think, *Well, if he feels lacking, how should the rest of us feel?* Do we even agree with the man that neglecting a time in prayer each day is "a criminal waste of time"?

Let's assume that *prayer is power*—for Luther Rice, for you, for me. The Greek word for power is *dunamis,* from which we get our word *dynamite.* Prayer is dynamite! It causes an explosion of divine energy. It moves things, even mountains! But a prayerless Christian is a powerless one.

Jesus said we "ought always to pray and not lose heart" (Luke 18:1). See how practical prayer is? You pray or you lose heart, one or the other. And you make the choice which way it's to be. Prayer does you good. Or better, through prayer God does for you the good He wanted to all along, but couldn't because you wouldn't let Him.

How serious is not praying? As serious as a drug addiction, or a tax audit, or a lawsuit that could ruin you. As serious as any surgery. It's something to get serious about.

Not praying is a sin, and possibly the basic sin. The one that leads to all the others. If people really prayed, would they sin as they do? Would they be hurtful and selfish as they are? *What if it all boils down to this, that sin keeps us from praying, or prayer keeps us from sinning, one or the other?*

This book is meant as practical help for people who want to grow in prayer. It has a simple plan. First it studies the example of the Model Prayer given by Christ. Then it proceeds through a series of lessons designed to create a learning experience. These may be done on an individual basis or in a group. Finally, there are written prayers which focus on life situations as suggested by various Scripture passages. These are suitable for family or private devotions, and may be useful also in worship and Bible study groups.

Silver Spring, Maryland

CONTENTS

Part I

From the Master Himself
──────The Model Prayer──────

Our Father who art in heaven, hallowed be thy name. Thy kingdom come, Thy will be done, on earth as it is in heaven. Give us this day our daily bread; and forgive us our debts, as we also have forgiven our debtors; and lead us not into temptation, but deliver us from evil. For Thine is the kingdom and the power and the glory, for ever. Amen (Matt. 6:9-13).

With so many questions always surrounding us, it's strange how the big ones never seem to get asked. I'm a pastor, and people are always after me about things—sometimes two or three at once! "Who's the chairman of the so-and-so committee?" "When did you say that meeting was?" "I heard Mr. Miller's in the hospital, what's the matter?" The list goes on and would bore you to death.

No one ever walks up and says: "Pastor, if I die will I live again?" Although that's more crucial. And it is on people's minds, isn't it? So why don't we ask questions like that? Why play games all the time?

Or take this one: "What must I do to be saved?" That comes right out of the Bible. And isn't it a question on many people's minds? But how often is it asked?

Or what about "How can I learn to pray"? That was the disciples' question which resulted in the giving of the Model Prayer. And it's to their credit that they asked it. Jesus likely knew it was on their minds, but it shows something about you when you can ask.

There's a joke in my family about asking directions while

traveling. I pride myself on being able to find places without
help. Even if it takes me an extra hour to do it! But my father,
who sometimes travels with us, was always prone to "stop at
a filling station and ask." So when he detects some uncertainty
in my route, he'll sometimes make that suggestion. And I always tell him "Thanks, but I don't think I need to." And my
wife and daughter just shake their heads!

This is a game we play, of course, and no great harm is done.
But harm is done when we are too proud or stubborn or shy or
thoughtless to get around to asking about the main directions
of life like those twelve saying, "Teach us to pray."

Maybe it can be said that a person who holds in his hand a
book on prayer has done about the same thing! An initiative
has been taken, a need confessed, an inquiry begun. I commend
you, good reader! So let's get started. The Model Prayer seems
an appropriate place.

But here I must tell you a problem. The problem is that you
know this prayer too well! You know it so well it's hard to look
at it fresh again. From its opening words, the mind slips into
a groove like a phonograph needle. The computer of long experience takes over, and you don't hear much afterward. You
can get around that, but you'll have to try very hard.

I have a friend who's worked most of his life at the Govern-
ment Printing Office in Washington, D.C. His job is proofread-
ing. All day long he reads to find mistakes in things before they
go to press. He told me a secret. He said you begin by starting
at the back and reading word by word to the front. You do that
with every sentence. That way, he said, your mind can't assume
anything about what a word was supposed to be. You'll be less
likely to look at a "thes" and see it as "this" because that's what
the context calls for.

In like manner, you must take a good long look at the Model
Prayer. Try to do it without all your preconceptions. Read it
backwards if you need to! Imagine yourself as one of the twelve,
maybe even the one who said, "Teach us to pray" (Luke 11:1)
and hear it for the very first time.

Remember it was given as a guide. That's what their question called for, didn't it? The prayer was a teaching device in the truest sense. What a sad misuse of the Lord's intention when it's taken and said by rote as the only prayer a lot of people ever pray. Instead, it was given as a "stimulus prayer"—something to prime the pump. It was an outline to be taken over and filled in with our own list of needs.

In the Sermon on the Mount, where the prayer is placed in Matthew's Gospel, Jesus had poked fun at prayers used for showing-off. He said avoid that, and spoke instead in terms of a closet. "Enter your closet," he said, "shut the door, and pray to your heavenly Father who sees you in secret" (see Matt. 6:6).

That saying may account for a certain reluctance in most of us. It seems to put prayer in the most private of all realms. Perhaps we shouldn't talk about it with other people or try to analyze it very much.

There's a point there to consider. On the other hand we do need help and encouragement, even with some of our most personal and private problems! At any rate, those who heard the Sermon on the Mount felt it was OK to ask help with their praying and to talk about it together. And Jesus went along. He said "Sure, I'll show you how." So they listened and then tried it themselves. And now it's our turn.

Let's look at what He gave them. Let's look at it as a whole before we examine its various parts:

> *Our Father who art in heaven* ["Father," we say, as if we have every right to] *hallowed by thy name* [by which we mean, dear Lord, that our greatest love and respect for anyone is for you. That you're the most special of all the special people in our lives]. *Thy kingdom come, Thy will be done on earth as it is in heaven* [which is twice now that heaven's been mentioned—first as the place where you dwell, then as a place where everything is good and holy. Which isn't here where I live, is it Lord? Ah, but someday . . . maybe? Could it be?]. *Give us this day our daily bread* [or maybe this week I'll need help with Exxon or AT&T

even more, or something strong for a headache, or a little
break at the tax assessor's office, or cool weather till the
air conditioner gets fixed, or . . .? You don't *mind* that kind
of asking do you Lord?] *And forgive us our trespasses as we
forgive those who trespass against us* [or should it be that
plainer word—*sin. My* sins, which are many and sometimes very heavy. Too much for me to cope with, but not
for you, thank heaven!] *And lead us not into temptation,
but deliver us from evil* [which shows we fear the future,
doesn't it? The past has been hard enough, surely there's
a better day ahead. Surely we've been tested enough, seen
evil enough. Deliver us from that, we pray!] (vv. 9-13).

Now I know that paraphrases it quite a bit, but I think you
have to do so. I think it was meant for that. Jesus wasn't saying,
"Here, take this and pray this." He was saying "Listen to this
and pray like this." We must take it seriously; we must make
it our pattern without enshrining the words themselves. The
pattern is what's intended for our use.

My prayer and yours could be, for us, a better prayer than
the Model Prayer itself! (Is the roof well supported?) That's
what a model is for. Our own prayer can be better in the sense
that it reflects our own life situation. But it will still need to
follow the pattern to do that, so we begin with with the pattern.

Let's take a shorter look, and then a longer look.

For the quick look, I want to describe five "movements" in
the Model Prayer. The first is what I call *THE GLORY*—the
"Hallowed be thy name." Prayer begins with God, you see, not
with us. Reverence is its first requirement. The most awkward
human pose is self-conceit. And if that's a bad thing in our
human dealings, how much worse it is as an attitude expressed
to God. The Bible calls it blasphemy, in fact. So humility is a
requirement of prayer, because only out of that comes the
praise of God's greatness which gets a prayer started.

A second movement of the prayer is *THE LONGING*. A longing for the kingdom to come so that earth becomes like heaven!

So that everywhere you travel you'd find people living in the perfect will of God. That's some longing!

Effectual prayer needs some burden to carry, some imperative, some fire in the bones. Let others be passive and accepting of things as they are, we mustn't! We must wrestle with the issues of that great gulf between the actual and the ideal. We must dream of what is possible with the help of God.

As we pray more about those issues, we'll find ourselves more and more involved in efforts to being them about, as were the followers of Jesus when told to pray for an increase in the labor force of His harvest. They became the answer to their very own prayers, it turned out! Which is what the Lord had in mind all the time. But that was only possible because they'd had a longing for it all the while.

The third movement of the prayer might be called *THE PRACTICUM*—the prayer for practical, daily necessities—bread, in other words.

For Martin Luther, the bread here stood for "everything necessary to the support and comfort of existence, as food and raiment, house and land, money and goods, a kind spouse, good children, faithful servants, righteous magistrates, good weather, peace, health, honor, true friends, good neighbors, and the like."[1]

Now if Luther's idea makes sense, it also makes sense to suggest, as he might well approve, that Christianity is the most worldy of all religions. It has such a strong emphasis on material things. The body is a temple of the Holy Spirit, the Bible says. And wherever Christians have gone they've tried to do things with bodies. They've healed sick ones, clothed naked ones, fed hungry ones, given water to thirsty ones, and the list goes on. Those, you see, are "down-to-earth" matters. The Gnostics were afraid of them, but we should not be. In the example of our Lord, they become profoundly holy.

Then comes the fourth movement of the prayer, which I call *THE UNBURDENING*—the forgiveness of sins. Of all the things that weigh us down, the heaviest aren't the material ones we worry about so much, they're the spiritual things. Where *we know matters aren't right with our souls*. We know we need forgiving, often by one another, and always by God. Even when our daily bread is stacked around us in abundance, when we feel we're far ahead in the competition of life, it can be that way. As if man can not live by bread alone.

Unburdening is hard. Robert Louis Stevenson walked out of a meeting once. When his wife asked him why, he said: "It is this: I am not yet fit to say 'Forgive us our trespasses as we forgive those who trespass against us.'"[2]

The last movement of the prayer is what I call *THE WEARINESS*. It says "Do not bring us to the test; deliver us from evil." Which sounds like someone hard-pressed and wanting a little peace, doesn't it? This is no phony business with the stuck-on smile and the movie-star suit and the idea that being a Christian means you're always on top of things. Sometimes things are on top of you ("O Jerusalem, Jerusalem," He cried), and you must ask for *deliverance* from them. With that you have the stark but realistic ending to this prayer the Master gave.

One other general observation before we begin looking in detail: *the prayer has something like a cloud of threat hanging over it.* Yes, threat. So that its constant theme is *struggle*.

Look and see. "Hallowed be Thy name" implies the fact that the Lord's name is dishonored by many, isn't hallowed by them. "Thy kingdom come" shows it hasn't come yet, and doesn't look much like it is right at the moment. "Give us our daily bread" is there because of constant threats to our existence. "Forgive us" is there because spiritual danger is constant about us, because "my sin is ever before me" (Ps. 51:3). And "lead us not into temptation" (or "testing") shows failure and ruin are out there waiting to get us, and without the intervening help of the Lord we're bound to lose out in the struggle.

So there's little ease in this prayer. The situation of our lives is like Christ telling the disciples, "Watch and pray that you may not enter into temptation" (Matt. 26:41). That was a late hour in Gethsemane, and a certain weariness was on them all.

And they did enter into temptation, and were not delivered from its evil; not that night, at least. They forsook Him and fled. In His hour of greatest need, they left Him alone and destitute. So later they had a lot of "unburdening" to do. One of them even hanged himself. And the point I make in all this is simply that the Model Prayer locates us all in a similar state of desperate need and constant threat.

Our English word for *prayer* literally means "to ask," and that gives us away. For all too many people, that's all prayer means. It's how you get something you want. It's a totally selfish thing. There's no denying prayer that includes asking and receiving, but to exclude by our overasking such things as praise, thanksgiving, confession, and intercession is to practice a vile corruption indeed.

It's something like this: asking and receiving in prayer is like the dessert. We naturally look forward to it and enjoy it. But that makes it tempting to overindulge, and many people do. They get a spiritual (from their point of view) sweet tooth! All the Lord ever hears from them is "give me this, give me that, give me something else"—and on and on.

Following the pattern of the Model Prayer will help us with that problem. It has six petitions (some count seven), and only three of those ask personal help, and they come last!

But how are we to think of the God to whom our prayers are addressed? Is He close to us or far away? Is He right there with us on our level or towering high above us? Is He an intimate friend to relax and let your hair down with, or is He a King before whom we must bow and keep silence?

Actually the answer is no simple yes or no, it's something of both. The Model Prayer implies that in the very opening line, where we call God our Father in heaven. *Father* implies closeness and intimacy; while *heaven* implies distance, separateness, and transcendence (as the theologians say). The prayer, as it unfolds, will move from concerns that are large and universal to others that are small and of local significance.

The point is this: He is the Lord of life. He's both "there" and "here." With Him we're but specks of dust among uncounted stars, yet He knows the number of hairs on our head. I admit this is hard to grasp, but the effort toward doing so is important. I wish I were able to express it better.

Whichever of those concepts of God is the harder for you to grasp, that's the one you need to work on. There are people whose object of worship is a high and lofty God, but they know Him in no warm or personal way. And others speak of God much like they do their hairdresser or favorite television star. Neither point of view is totally wrong, but each could use a dose of the other to make it better.

Taken broadly, the Model Prayer begins with a theology of life, then moves on to the particulars of its daily routine. Not a bad pattern. With that in mind, we'll begin our closer look at the prayer itself.

Hallowed Be Thy Name

"Hallowed be thy name"—what does it matter about names?

The answer is, it matters much. In a sense, the sum of everything known about a person gets embodied in his name. So when we enter Henry Aaron or O. J. Simpson in a "hall of fame" somewhere, we're saying a sort of "hallowed be thy name." Their name has been raised to a new level. The man feels good, and so do all his friends. It seems right. And to a lesser but not different degree, this is what occurs in the hanging of the pictures of past grand masters of the local lodge, or the giving of ribbons to members of the sixth-grade swim team.

Doesn't all the emotion of what we know about a person get lodged in the hearing or saying of his name? What do you feel when the name Richard Nixon is mentioned? Something for sure. Or Martin Luther King? Or Jerry Falwell? Or Jane Fonda? Or the most obnoxious gossip you know personally?

There is a difference between Billy Martin and Billy Graham, isn't there? They share a common name, but a different feeling comes. Even with brothers of the same family like Teddy, Robert, and John F., whatever the difference there is one.

And the name is the trigger—the name calls it back into memory. Don't ever say names aren't important. (By the time you get this book, the examples used may have faded some, they always do, but others will have taken their places—they always do.)

We compare names, and we rank them. We analyze and argue and say this one's better than that one. And by this we don't mean the name itself, of course, but the person it stands for. We even do this with persons dead and gone from the human scene. We settle on names above other names.

You see how that relates to the opening of the Model Prayer, don't you? To say "Hallowed be *thy* name" is to give God His due. It's to recognize Him as who He is. It means we know His name, and know it's a name so different in kind that in its presence any other name is bound to be a lesser one. It's a name that was before all other names, and on which all others depend for their existence. It's a name destined to be spoken when all others fall silent—an Eternal Name.

What can we do with our hallowed-be-thy-names but give them to that Name?

We're being shown how a proper prayer begins. We're being told that unless we have that recognition of God's name in us we'll never pray much. We may move our mouths and wag our tongues and form words, but they won't be a prayer. That sounds like overstatement, but I don't think it is.

Here, then, is the first and great petition. It's first because it puts God first, as He must be with those who are His sons and daughters. George Buttrick paraphrased it as follows: "Our Father, cause Thine eternal nature, revealed in Christ, to be hallowed by us and by all men."[3]

Now although this sounds like "church talk," the worst that could happen would be its confinement there. A reverence for God as God must infuse one's daily life and daily consciousness. Work, play, business, speech, friendships, family life—all of it. For it's in those realms that all too often we take God's name in vain. And by that I don't mean "cussing," I mean failing to give Him His due.

All this is far more a matter of the heart than anything else. You can learn it like a lesson and it stays a lesson learned. You can say it like a doctrine and it stays a doctrine said. It has kinship with music and with poetry. It is something caught more than something taught.

That states the point made by Rudolph Otto in his famous classic, *The Idea of the Holy.*[4] He admits we'll always be trying to express our idea of God in rational words. But then he adds: "We have to predicate them on a subject which they qualify, but which in its deepest essence is not, nor indeed can be, comprehended in them; which rather requires comprehension of a quite different kind."

Otto wrote of what he termed the "mysterium tremendum" (tremendous mystery), and of our "hushed, trembling, and speechless humility . . . in the presence of . . . that which is a mystery inexpressible and above all creatures."[5]

This "need of the holy" is deep rooted in every human being and part of what is meant by the "image of God" (Gen. 1:27). It's connection with prayer is that prayer gives expression to it and satisfies a part of its requirement. So prayer isn't something God needs from us, but something we have great need to express to Him. We have a deep and abiding hunger within, a "God-shaped void."

There are things besides prayer that try to fill that void. There are counterfeits. There are entertainments and diversions and false pieties galore. There are witch doctors and home remedies. There are even civic clubs and fraternal orders. In fact, *anything* in life may be used temporarily as a substitute for God. But what will be left at last is only a great and gnawing emptiness.

You can say then, and be perfectly true, that prayer is extremely *practical* in nature. If the practical is defined as what's needful, workable, and useful in our lives, what could be more practical? But how often is "Hallowed be thy name" given credit as such? In most minds, it's a nice, pretty saying, associated with soft lights and organ music and people reciting in chorus. It certainly is no key to living. And thus does modern, secular man go stumbling on to the worship of what he calls "the practical."

Nothing is quite as sad as seeing this so-called practical person in the throes of life's extremity, where his cherished and hard-fought practicalities have all run out. Where, all of a sudden, the Persian rugs on the floor and the private-school diplomas on the wall and the carefully planned insurance programs mean nothing. And I don't suggest this only applies to the successful and affluent. It applies to anyone who lives in neglect of "Hallowed be thy name."

You see it in their faces. All of a sudden the things they valued are valueless, their practicalities impractical. There's confusion and unaccustomed desperateness. There's often a hasty effort to go back and start all over again. But the latecomer has problems. A lifetime of prayer neglected is hard to catch up in a few pressured minutes.

So ultimately its what the heart holds, not the hands, that matters most. Fewer ribbons on the wall, perhaps. Less treasure on earth and more in heaven. Less I and more Thou. That sounds like preaching, I know, but isn't it the truth? What then is a proper hallowing?

Whatever it is, it more depends on an adoring heart than a polished tongue. I say that as a "word man" myself. But if we speak with tongues of men and angels and don't have a true love of God, it profits us nothing. And its deadliest enemy is the hypocrisy that pretends it.

Also this is a personal thing with every soul. *No one can pray your "Hallowed be thy name" for you.* And I don't mean you might not use someone else's words. But they have to become *your* words first. They have to become yours and belong to you as surely as they were someone else's first. All else is vanity.

To pray "Hallowed by thy name" is to change our agenda. The name we naturally hallow most is our own. We build it up, defend it against attack, and love to hear it spoken above all others. Now, however, another name takes center stage. The rule of self-concern is broken. We're saying something like this:

> *Your* name, O God—Your name above my own. Your name instead of my own. Your name before and after my own. Your name as the hope of mine.

We must get the idea of something *unconditional* here. Prayer is more than a religious business where we suggest to the Almighty that both of us can prosper in a partnership arrangement. We scratch His back and He scratches ours. Draw up a deal and shake hands on it. Phooey! It's more like this: "Not my will, but thine, be done" (Luke 22:42). It could even be like it was with Job, crying "Though he slay me, yet will I trust in him"(13:15, KJV).

There really are no other choices, though indeed there may seem to be. But living in the spirit of this prayer, we find it's all we need.

Thy Kingdom Come

As we move to the second part of the Model Prayer let me stress the point made earlier about its "unselfishness." Standing here at milepost two, we're still a long way from getting to where we pray about our selfish concerns. The time for reminding the Lord about our need for daily bread will come, but it isn't yet. We must dwell longer with *His* business, not *ours*.

We once had a guest in our home for part of an afternoon. He was a "friend of a friend," and the friend seemed anxious for us to meet and get to know him. Since he was also a minister and from overseas, it seemed like a good idea. The country he was from held a lot of interest for me, and after we were introduced I proceeded to ask question after question. He proved very articulate, and in over an hour of conversation I found out much about his country, and much about *him*.

Only there was something funny about that afternoon. In all that time, this stranger asked not a word about *me*. Where I was from, where I went to school, how long I'd been pastor of my church, where I may have traveled, anything about my views on this or that—nothing, zero. As I said, the man was articulate about himself and his views on things, so it wasn't that he didn't know how to frame a question. It appeared that he simply had no interest. It was the most striking example in my conversational experience of an individual totally preoccupied with himself and indifferent to the person on the other end of of the thing.

What has that to do with prayer? We're often inclined to do the very same with God. We come before His throne of grace and speak only about ourselves! We come with a list in our hand saying, "Here's what I want today" or "Here's how I feel today" or "Here's what I thank you for today, Lord." And the focus of it all is the "I," you see. We basically ignore Him except in how He can serve our needs, or has. He must think us very rude! Now on to the second petition, "Thy kingdom come."

Whose kingdom are we concerned with most of the time? You know it, tell me. Our own of course. Even as we speak the language of religion, it's often our own kingdom we're seeking to build. We're in the religion business for what we can get out of it. So the prayer closest to actual practice is a prayer that says, let "*my* kingdom come!"

Not that we actually put it in those words, of course. But we pray as if we're the number one thing. Not God, not His kingdom, but us. We want His help to get things fixed up and settled in our lives. The house, the job, the car, the kids, even people who pester and aggravate us. It's a natural enough desire. But it forgets that we're strangers and pilgrims on this earth and seeking a better country. It acts as if the here and now is *it*.

The Model Prayer will have us stay longer in the realm of larger concerns. The accent is on *thy*.

> *Thy* name be hallowed, *thy* kingdom come, *thy* will, O God, be done.

Jesus knew how hard it is to concern ourselves that broadly. Like camels going through the eye of needles, that's what. The instinctive thing is to look down at things of earth, not up toward the things of heaven. The Lord may have meant that in His language of "Lift up your eyes, and look on the fields that are ripe to harvest."

What happens if you don't lift up your eyes? Your world of concern stays bounded by the small diameters of earthly travel. You remain an earthbound creature. You say the words, but never really pray the prayer, "Thy kingdom come."

How *does* the kingdom come? Paul said, "The kingdom of God is . . . righteousness and peace and joy in the Holy Spirit" (Rom. 14:17). In that sense, God's kingdom comes every time His Spirit gains welcome in someone's heart. In that sense, the kingdom is accurately defined as "the rule and reign of God in the human heart." So we may say the second petition has something to do with evangelism. We're praying that persons will be saved who now are lost. Where would it leave us if that prayer had to be answered before our prayer for daily bread?

I realize the word *evangelism* leaves a bad taste in some mouths, and I know some of the evangelists who've helped make that so! But woe to us if we mind our own souls and care nothing for the souls of others. And woe to us if we give cups of water in the Master's name and never speak of the Master Himself who has living water to give.

Remember what was said earlier about being the answer to your own prayers? Here's a place where that applies as much as any other. You put yourself on the spot when you pray, "Thy kingdom come." God now has a right to watch you *help* it come! And you can't hire that duty out to professionals, as some people like to think. It's a personal task you accept as part of your participation in the family of God.

That we "lift up our eyes and look" is implied as the outcome of this petition. It's goes something like this:

> Let your kingdom come, O God—to him, and to her, and to them, and in the realization of its fullness let it come more and more to me.

Buttrick called this petition "a blowing of trumpets and an unfurling of banners."[6] Too few of us are into trumpets and banners.

Of course, there's human freedom to account for here. Our Father in heaven has here on this earth a lot of very unruly children! So to pray for His rule and reign over them is to pray about something *they* have a say in. Constantine took his emperor's sword and tried to threaten people into the kingdom, and it wasn't meant to work that way. Enticement and trickery don't work either. Nor do pressure and guilt and embarrassment, though they're often tried. A soul must respond freely to the love of God, who never chooses to coerce. And that puts the matter right back in the lap of prayer.

Maybe we should say *fervent* prayer. For the power isn't the saying of nice words, but the personal passion of praying, "Thy kingdom come." We must really want it to come, to others and to us.

That this lies in the realm of prayer should tip us off to something else. The kingdom of God, whatever it is, is something He establishes Himself. It's not something we establish for Him. We ask for it and hope for it, but then we *wait* for it. We do our part, but we know all the while that it lies beyond our doing. We play our little games in the process, but the big game is played with us.

Omar Khayyám put that in some rather pessimistic lines that still serve to make the point:

> But helpless Pieces of the Game He plays
> Upon this Checker-board of Nights and Days;
> Hither and thither moves, and checks, and slays,
> And one by one back in the Closet lays.
>
> The Ball no question makes of Ayes and Noes,
> But Here or There as strikes the Player goes;
> And He that toss'd you down into the field,
> He knows about it all—He knows—HE knows![7]

There are larger realms, then, which are touched only through prayer. "Thy kingdom come" has to do with them.

But it may have other meanings, too. Jesus spoke of the kingdom as a mixture of yeast in a lump of dough, or a mustard seed planted in the field. Those illustrate matters earthly and at hand. They also have to do with time's passing.

Think of those first disciples praying this prayer. After they organized as a church, they had to run from the Jews. Then later they had to run from Rome. They seemed always to be running from something. They were driven to caves and secret meetings in the night. It wasn't that they lacked courage to face their adversaries, they were simply too weak in worldly weapons. So they became a martyr church. And yet *this* was the church of Jesus which the gates of hell were not to prevail against!

All this time, though, they were praying, "Thy kingdom come." Yet it never seemed to. They moved from one persecution to the next, one setback to the next, and some became discouraged. Some even quit. What became of the prayer?

Today, Caesar's Rome is a thing of museums and history books, but the church is still here. It's even in countries like China and Russia, where for generations now other emperors have tried to put it out. Something has come of the prayer after all, has it not?

I don't imply that the matter is over and done with. We still have need to pray the prayer, and those who take our places will too. But I mean to say that God has been working His purpose out as year succeeds to year, and is doing it still today, and will be in the future.

Godless emperors still sit on thrones, and the kingdom hasn't come if it means pulling them all down. If it means a time when righteousness covers the earth as waters cover the sea, it hasn't come. But still, in true hearts everywhere, it *has*. I know it, and so do you. So someone's prayer sometime got a yes.

It *has* come, but yet it *is* coming—both statements are true in their own way. The lordship of Christ has begun, but isn't finished. Prayers of saints and martyrs have gotten answered, but some are still left. "Thy kingdom come"? It has, and it is, but it will be even more. We shouldn't make it sound easy, but we must always know it's *certain*.

The Bible ends with a strange and wondrous book we call "The Revelation of John." It has much to do with the kingdom of God. Throughout most of its pages, the kingdom is engaged in fearful struggles. Evil and evildoers abound. Even the love of saints has turned lukewarm. But the writer makes it quite plain that though the struggle may be long, the issue is never in doubt.

The Lord God omnipotent reigneth—that's how things end up. Right here and now now He reigns for some, but one day He'll reign over all. Through human history the kingdom has often seemed trifling indeed, but a day is coming when all who trifled with it will be sorry they did.

The beauty of God's original creation will be restored in a new heaven and a new earth, and sighing and sorrow will flee away. There'll be no more pain or sickness or evil of any kind. The kingdom is coming in its fullness at last, triumphant and eternal at history's end. "Amen. Come, Lord Jesus!" (Rev. 22: 20).

Do you see now what a mighty and significant prayer this is?

Thy Will Be Done

Over the years, I've noticed how things we preach to others have a way of coming back at us from the rear. It's as if a heavenly scribe takes notes when we begin pontificating, marks it on some grand calendar, then has us put to the test to see if that was something we really meant, or just talk.

Imagine Jesus of Nazareth, sitting in the shade of a tree, His admirers gathered around Him for the Sermon on the Mount. They've asked Him for a lesson in praying, and He's said, "Well, you do it like this. . . ." And among the items He covers is one about the will of God being done on earth as it is in heaven. Pray for that, He tells them. They all nod their heads.

Now skip some years. Go past the woman at the well and the death of Lazarus. Go on toward the cross. Go to that garden where they gathered after Judas left to betray Him. There He waited and prayed. There the agony of the next day loomed large ahead of Him. He was there in some fear. He was there in frustration and uncertainty. He was there with an urge to quit the whole thing while the quitting was good. *What would His prayer be at a time like that?*

It was easier to speak of praying "Thy will be done" back there in those happier days, wasn't it? Now, in the clutches of this actual situation the stakes got higher. You see, you're never sure what you or anyone else will do about a problem till then. All idle talk that begins, "Well, if I were her, I'd do so-and-so" is suspect. It's too cheap and easy. Jesus *did* pray the same prayer in Gethsemane He'd taught in the Model Prayer: "Not my will, but thine, be done." But now it's a much different situation.

The language here is the language of *submission,* isn't it? Someone with a will of His own defers to the will of another. Think of that.

The push of our society these days is in the opposite direction. Submission is out and assertion is in. Glenn Hinson called attention to this in his book *The Reaffirmation of Prayer.* He said, "If we recover the prayer of surrender, we will have to fly directly in the face of the principle of aggressiveness which characterizes our society."[8]

The Bibles of the modern world are books like Robert Ringer's *Winning Through Intimidation* and *Looking Out for #1.* They argue that the enemy of our happiness is moral restraint. They say we shouldn't feel all those debts to other people—let others look out for themselves. Forget about duties that bring no return, just seek your pleasure. And don't let anybody stand in your way of doing it.[9]

The incentive system of our culture is geared toward rewarding those who demand their due. Work on your drive and ambition to get what you want. After you've gotten that, you can go after something even bigger. Anyone can do it—only suckers don't! And the prayer of that way of life is quite simple: *"My will be done."*

This could be why Americans love professional sports so avidly. We get those extremely strong-willed individuals, determined to win at all cost, paid outrageously to do so, and put them against one another where only one can win and the other must go home a loser. We make them butt heads and see who wants it the most. And that's only a parable of the contests going on daily in the streets and homes and offices of the land.

Do you see, then, what an odd thing is a prayer that calls for us to say, "Not my will, but thine, be done"?

Of course you can pull the claws of that prayer. You can rationalize it and make it tame and harmless if you've a mind to. Make you a god in the image of your own ambition, a success god. That one often gets prayed to at businessmen's luncheons. A sort of fix-me-up-and-bless-me god.

This model prayer isn't as tame as it sounds! In fact it's downright dangerous and radical. To pray to a real and living God that His will be done is no slight thing if you mean it!

The language here implies a conflict. We want one thing and God wants another. Why else pray a prayer of surrender to *His* will? Flesh and spirit have a war with one another, as Paul often pointed out. So it's quite a thing to say, "Lord, let what You want prevail, not what I want."

Sometimes we may know very well what God wants, and other times we may not. I'm not sure how it was there in Gethsemane. The Bible clearly shows it as a place of agony, which can mean a "valley of decision." If Jesus *knew* the Father's will, then His struggle was submitting to it. But perhaps the struggle was to know in the first place. Or maybe both?

He began by praying, "Take this cup from me." But that was not to be. In a sense, that was a failed prayer. And after it came the second prayer, "Thy will be done." All of which shows how hard it is at times to know what the will of the Father is. Rarely can we know exactly what God wants the second we want to know it.

That fact makes prayer all the more vital. We don't have to know the answers to much to pray, "Thy will be done." We may see no way out. We may be unsure what God has in mind. But we can come to Him in such a prayer saying: "Here I am Lord. I'm willing, even if it's hard. I submit to what You want, even without knowing for sure what it is." There you have the meaning of the word *faith!*

One ought to speak such words with a smile on one's face and hope in one's heart. "Thy will be done" finds itself all to often in company with the sigh and the put-down look. The chin droops and the lower lip sticks out. As if all we want is contrary to all God wants, but now and then He forces the issue and we have to let Him have His way. We behave like spoiled children.

Something is wrong with that. The realm of the kingdom was supposed to be a realm of joy. It's supposed to be a pearl merchant finding the pearl he's always wanted and eagerly selling all he has to buy that one. He wasn't sorry about what he had to sell. He forgot all that in the exuberance of this new age begun in his life! Try to remember that when you pray, "Thy will be done." It might not be so bad after all.

This isn't to say the will of the Lord isn't hard at times. But remember what Proverbs 13 says about the alternative? It says, "The way of the transgressor is hard!" I suppose you take your choice. "As for me and my house. . . ."

Hard as it may often be, there's joy in obedience to the will of God. It may be the joy of hard effort; it may even mean suffering. But recall that remarkable statement in the Letter to the Hebrews:

> *He for the joy that was set before him endured the cross* (12:2).

The harder thing is often the better thing, and there's joy to be had along the way if it belongs to the will of God.

"Thy will be done" should be thought of as *the fundamental*

prayer. If we could have but one, this ought to be it; that God's
will be done with us, right now in this moment of our thought
about it, and tonight when we close our eyes, and until when-
ever is until, and even after.

We're at a great divide here. Many people are interested in
religion as an intellectual pursuit. They have no intention of
kneeling down before God and praying for His will to be done
in their lives. They operate as if the key is in knowing things.
But remember the prayer isn't "thy will be known," it's "thy
will be *done.*" The last thing God needs is a lot of smart opinions
on this and that!

In addition to its obvious meaning for an individual's life, the
same prayer has meaning for the life of society as well. I give
you an example:

> There are a lot of dug holes in this earth, all concreted
> and tiled and covered up on top. Inside them, someone in
> uniform sits surrounded by dials and lights and telephones
> and switches. And a huge hulk of warhead and missile
> rests there, too, which is the business of the place. And it
> can unleash sudden death on millions of earth's own, more
> than were ever struck at one blow before, more than were
> even alive through most of history. It sits there through
> the days and nights . . . waiting.

How does "Thy will be done" apply to that place? To all such
places? And to plans we and others have to build them more
and more, and even deadlier? Surely, we think about it. Should
we pray as well? Do we dare pray "Thy will be done," even for
a place like that?

The prayer has its *social* side. Thy will be done, O Lord, for
parents whose children ran away. And for cancer-causing stuff
that gets in the air we breathe. And for people out of jobs whom
no one is going to hire. And for courtrooms where child custo-
dies are decided while people weep. And for California if the big
earthquake comes. And for farmers who'll fail if the rain

doesn't come. And for airliners with tiny cracks in their engine mounts.

That's only a start, of course. But do you see how much praying there needs to be?

Give Us This Day Our Daily Bread

Finally we've come to the *good* part!

But seriously, one should see what a large jump is taken as you go from "Thy will be done" to "Give us this day our daily bread." It's as if those otherworldly and religious concerns are put behind us, and it's beans and eggs and milk that matter now. It's as if the practical has "done in" the profound, lesser things have taken the place of greater things, the divine has fallen victim to the worldly and mundane. And *Jesus* is to blame for this?

Though I'm speaking tongue-in-cheek, Christian interpreters have actually had a problem here, and some have gone scurrying off in search of explanations for this bread other than the obvious and literal one. Some have claimed this is a way of speaking of the Lord's Supper. "Give us our daily bread" means let us be in church that Sunday when they cover up the table with the big white cloth! Others have found here a code word which represents Christ as the Bread of heaven for our souls—something more "spiritual," you see.

Beware of those who tell you things like that. They're the kin of others who're always trying to rob Christ of His humanity, saying, "He couldn't have been human like us—He only pretended to be." As if God's too "spiritual" to have lived in a body like ours, doing all the things that bodies do.

The early church did frequent battle with that idea and finally branded it heresy. They decided God cares about our bodies, just as He cares about our souls. They accepted the statement that our bodies are the temple of His Holy Spirit.

I made a point earlier about the "worldliness" of the Christian religion.[10] One who studies the New Testament can see, for instance, that Jesus spent a lot of time in His ministry dealing with bodies. He straightened bent and crippled ones, touched lonely ones, fed hungry ones, healed diseased ones, stopped blood flowing out of hemorrhaging ones, refused to avoid contact with leprous ones, and so on. You really could make a long list. So we shouldn't be surprised at a prayer about bread from *Him*.

I remember praying of the Lord's Prayer in church as a boy and thinking, even then, that the part about daily bread seemed bothering the Lord about something that wasn't a problem! Our family wasn't rich, but we had food, and, especially, bread. Everyone in our town had food. On Saturdays the farmers hauled it to town by truckloads. So why pray about that?

The prayer wasn't getting through. It got translated as something like this: "Lord, make me truly grateful for this bread I'm bound to receive. And, if it please You, don't let there be any peas or spinach with it tonight. Then I can more heartily ask of You to help me clean up my plate, which always pleases Mother. Amen."

But knowing now about the table of earth and its lack of bread, what a strange prayer that seems! Across it sits a child with face drawn, belly bloated, bones and body malnourished, and whose prayer is literally "give me this day my daily bread." And all around the world table it's the same: people praying for bread over empty plates, and with little hope of anything to fill them.

How strange, then, our praying this prayer which seems like a nonprayer to us. Bread holds no urgency for us—we've never had a lack. This then is our forced and lackless prayer as far as its literal meaning is concerned. There are other meanings, though, as we'll see shortly.

Isn't the *us* of this petition of great significance? In fact, a major point of true religion is the movement from *me and mine* to *us and ours*. So we come to see ourselves as sitting around a table which has but one world family, and Christ Himself is the host and presider.

Only when we've prayed the *us* with that as its scope have

we prayed it right. Only then can God bless us as children who know how things are. It then is no longer us North Americans or South Americans or Asians or Africans. It's "give *us*, O Lord, all of us who live on Your earth—give us this day our daily bread."

By the way, did you notice the word *give?* That's the first time we've seen it in the Model Prayer. Also it'll be the last. But it's there, sure enough—give us something, Lord! He's the giver, and we're the givees. We're dependents and supplicants.

Other times in prayer, other times in this prayer, we seek spiritual blessings. Here, though, we seek bread. We don't live by bread alone, but we do live by it partly.

Wait a minute, though, someone said we *worked* for bread. They call some of us, more of us now, "breadwinners." So what's this about it being given? And didn't God say to Adam that he'd have to earn it by the sweat of his brow? And didn't Paul write later on that "If a man will not work, neither let him eat"? So the question is, do we work to eat, or pray to eat?

That may seem like a trick question, but bear with it for a minute. Remember how Jesus once gave instruction to "watch and pray"? Those seem to contradict, but actually they go hand in hand. They also suggest "work and pray," which is somewhat the answer to our question. He who prays without working is a spiritual fool, but whoever works without praying will eventually lose all his work. He may tear down his barns and build bigger ones to hold his profit, but a voice will come and call him a fool. It will ask him "then whose shall those things be?" (Luke 12:20, KJV). And he will tremble at the meaning of "then."

So we must be neither nonworking pray-ers, nor nonpraying workers. The two belong together. We pray "Thy kingdom come" with a willingness to help it come, and we pray for daily bread in the same spirit. We do so as workmen, sowers, gatherers, and sharers with others in need.

Though this is a kind of "gimme prayer," we need to bear in mind the simplicity of it. "Give us our daily bread" is a long way from "give me a condo at the beach, and a new Mercedes to drive back and forth!" It seems to imply a basic sort of life-style, as basic as bread itself. Reflect on the words of the great apostle who urged some of his more affluent followers: "Having food and raiment let us be therewith content"(1 Tim. 6:8, KJV).

God isn't Santa Claus. He won't take it kindly if we act like spoiled children, grabbing up all the presents in sight and hiding them from one another.

If you look at it in that light, "Give us our daily bread" may be more revolutionary than it seemed at first. It asks only for what's needed to sustain us. It doesn't cater to the list-making impulses of our covetousness. If taken seriously and literally, it would surely result in there being more to go around. Think about that as you pray.

Notice also that the prayer is for God's help with our earthly needs *as we meet up with them*. "Give us our *daily* bread." It doesn't ask for more than a day at a time. It's better that we stay in a relationship of daily dependence on the goodness and provisions of God.

That raises the matter of our vulnerability. None of us lives unto himself or within himself. We must have bread, some every day, or soon we die. We're bound to this earth by that fact, and to others of this earth who're similarly bound, and, finally, to God Himself as our only true sustenance.

How else can we have bread? First the grain, then the blade, then the full corn in the ear. The Lord must water it and nourish it and shower His sunshine down upon it. And others must go out in fields on our behalf, again and again. They must harvest it, carry it, grind and bake it—all before we hold it in our hands to eat. Do you see how we're beggars for bread?

We're forced by this prayer to consider the question of the source of things, and the answer isn't obvious. In a way, "Give us bread" seems misdirected. What has God to do with it anyway? Don't we get bread from markets, bakers, inns, neighbors, quick-stop places, and all the rest?

Ah, but that process is deceptive. The Lord who made heaven and earth sustains its operation daily, though not visibly. "In him we live and move and have our being" (Acts 17:28). Every peaceful day we spend, our life or death depends on whether God allows that day or not—though we obviously assume it. The prayer is meant to help us quit assuming.

The facing of our vulnerability and the acknowledging of this relationship to the Father is the agenda of all true prayer. It may be that we'll be given the day's bread, prayer or not. Many obviously are, for the Lord is gracious. Though other times that prayer could make a difference in having bread or not. But in either case a greater need hangs in the balance: that we bow daily before the truth of our fragile existence, hoping thereby to live in greater harmony with the wisdom behind it.

Is there any better place for beginning to know that than with bread? The meaning of the kingdom we may not know, but bread we do. Knowing how to hallow the name of God may be hard, but asking for bread is easy. If we can learn to relate to God on this rather basic level, it may help us move on to others.

The earth is the Lord's and the fullness thereof, the world and we who dwell therein. With Him a day is as a thousand years long, and a thousand years as short as a day with us. His ways are not our ways, or His thoughts our thoughts; they're high and beyond us, as heaven is. And yet every day He meets us in the bread we eat, or we meet Him, or both.

The name of our place is Emmaus. He is known to us here in the breaking of bread. Hold it in your hands. See how good it is. Enjoy.

But know surely that you'll be hungry again after you eat it. And soon. And back to the same need, and living again in the same dependence you were born to.

We never outgrow this dependence, and we forget it to our peril.

"So give us, O Lord God, give us this day our daily bread." We ought not ask for more, but we must not ask for less.

Forgive Us Our Sins

Once again, as between the third and fourth petitions, notice the transition that takes place between the fourth and fifth. We move from "give us our bread" to "forgive us our sins." That is some transition, is it not?

From bread on our tables to the cleansing of our souls—quite a difference. It's a leap from the simplest to the most complex, from the easy to the near impossible. We move from a need that sounds so secular we hardly think of it as spiritual, to one that's so spiritual we often rule it out of the world of the secular. Yet the two may be intertwined in as common a thing as an argument over dinner!

Food and forgiveness. Both are what you could call, with pun intended, "gut issues!"

"Give us ... forgive us"—aren't there people who act as if the point of life and God is the first but not the second? They want the Lord as *giver* but not *forgiver.* The list of things they'd like from God grows longer with every television commercial, but where's the list that begins "forgive us these trespasses"? And of those two lists, which is more vital to the soul's well-being?

It's tough to seek and gain forgiveness. It's tough, even on the human level. It's tough even when our self-interest would be served by seeking forgiveness. What if there's no self-interest to cause someone's saying "please forgive me"? What if there are just two separated friends with bad stuff between them— how easy is it for one to walk up to the other and seek forgiveness?

Have you had experience with that at all? Can you tell what inside us makes it such a big deal? What inside us makes it an issue in the first place? Has any street dog who bit another one ever gone and tried to apologize later? He feels no need to, you say. Right. But *why* is it he *doesn't* and we *do?*

When we've hurt another person, why do we feel guilt and soon wish we could take it all back some easy, painless way? Why can't we hurt one another, then laugh and forget it and go on our merry way? Could the answer be that we're made in the image of God, that when one of us bites another, there's accountability to Him?

That's it, I think. That's why a person who bites others as a habit of life and never says "forgive me" carries it like a load on his back. And no matter how many times a magazine or psychiatrist tells him it's OK and not to worry about it, *he still worries about it.* He still knows, from something deep inside him, that it *isn't* OK.

He knows he's sinned and needs forgiveness. He fears there's a God who'll someday do to him as he's been doing to others. And he needs to pray, but he doesn't quite know how. His is a spiritual dilemma.

You tell me, good reader, is that put too strongly, or not? Is there some easier gospel to handle matters like that in a cleaner, more painless way? Are there some that can eliminate the need of a prayer, "Forgive us our sins"?[11]

There are such gospels around, but would you want to trust one? Some are sold on television. "Jesus will make you happy and prosperous" seems to be their theme and promise. One hears music with a lively beat and the singers gaily dressed and smiling, but there's not a lot about personal repentance. Perhaps the same comment could be made about my preaching. It's no easy matter. In fact, it's called the way of the cross.

But those stormy turmoils inside us over the hurts we give others are a sure evidence that Whoever put them there intends to take the matter seriously. So it's self-destructive in the end if we make a habit of glossing over them. It ought to be written as a fact of human science that if we forgive not others their trespasses, neither will our Heavenly Father forgive ours. To live, and work, and get, and go about, and finally die unforgiving and unforgiven—that's the greatest human tragedy.

Dr. Karl Menninger, do you know him? A respected psychiatrist with a lifetime of professional service and impeccable credentials, he came to that same conclusion in a remarkable book called *Whatever Became of Sin?* In it he wrote like a tent-meeting evangelist about the failure of secular help to bring lasting spiritual cures. Menninger said that any formula that takes no account of God deals only superficially with human guilt. He said we must forgive and be forgiven.

Mrs. Adams loved her son Jimmy and thought he was just the cutest kid there was. Until high school. In high school Jimmy fell into some very bad ways, disgraced himself and his family, and strained or broke every constructive relationship he had in life—you know the story. He's away from home now, and once he's, more or less, tried to say he's sorry. But how many "I'm sorry's" does a thing like that take? How many would it take for that mother to forgive as if none of it ever happened? Does anyone know?

And Jimmy, what of him? His problem may be even greater. For Jimmy hates himself, and he carries that self-hatred to whatever new amusement he finds. He carries the great burden of needing to forgive himself. And even his mother might not be all that anxious to have him do it. From her standpoint, he deserves to suffer as he made her suffer. So how and when can Jimmy ever be rid of his past?

Do you see how tangled this problem of forgiveness is?[12] Both the saints who're sinned against and the sinners who sin have need to forgive, and for both it's hard. Harder for whom isn't always easy to say.

Women employees have suffered years of abuse in a male-dominated workplace. Some of it subtle, some not. Either way, it accumulates. Will they ever forgive? Will they ever be asked to? What if they aren't—what becomes of all the hate?

Husbands who cheat on wives, wives who cheat on husbands. How many "I'm sorry's" does it take to fix it back? And also, what's the spiritual state of someone who's heard an honest "I'm sorry" and sluffed it off?

In fact, with most situations of human conflict, how often do the sainthood and virtue all reside on one side of the argument? Even in a case like Jimmy and Mrs. Adams, to think back to that. The language used in the Model Prayer seems to have an awareness of this problem. It says "forgive *us* as *we* forgive."

The plural is the mode of choice. The forgiving is a thing we need to both give and get. Almost always.

Our usual need is to work at the giving of it. The getting will then take care of itself, according to Christ. Let me tell you something I've seen in this world. No one is lonelier than a self-righteous person who believes others owe him an apology and is sitting somewhere waiting to receive it. Like the older brother in the story of the prodigal son, such a person may sit there and wait an awfully long while, and who gets hurt as he does?

How precious little forgiveness there is in the world? How few prayers like Stephen's, who asked, as they rained down their stones on his head, "Lord, lay not this sin to their charge" (Acts 8:60). He died, but didn't he die better? And remember how a young man named Saul was there holding people's coats and heard what was said. Who could hear a thing like that and not be affected? Saul would be.

All of us hear blame and cursing where the issues of life are joined. Cars honking, lawsuits threatened, vengeance taken, dooms sealed, all of that. The world is full of that. But the world waits in awe and wonder to hear the uttering of this word *forgive.*

Why, I heard of a man who drove all the way from New York to Texas to say that one word for something done years ago. He'd carried it with him all that way between.

Our unspoken "forgive me's" add to life's load. And especially as it gets along, and we begin to think they might remain unsaid forever.

Don't suppose, though, that all we need to do is forgive *one another.* Not by any means. All sin is sin against God, no matter who else it involves. Consider that greatest of penitential outpourings, the fifty-first Psalm. The author is heard to pray: "Against thee, thee only, have I sinned, and done this evil in thy sight" (v. 4, KJV). He's saying his sin is against God only. And yet clearly it involved other people, too.

It's really quite hard to sin against God without sinning

against other people at the same time. We don't often just steal or lie in general. Instead, we sin against some victim, bear false witness against some neighbor. But in that process we sin against the Lord God, too. So the prayer of the psalmist illustrates how this Godward dimension predominates. And afterward our need of forgiveness with Him comes first of all.

The Model Prayer could possibly be misleading here because the words provided ask a general forgiveness. They say forgive us our sins whatever those might be. We must remember that what we have in the Model Prayer is simply an outline, a form with which we fill in the blanks. Nothing is easier than a casual asking for all our sins to be forgiven, with none of them in mind as we do.

If you find it easy and often that you pray "and Lord, forgive me of all my sins," please listen for a rumble of heavenly thunder and a voice asking in reply: *"What sins?"* A tempting answer might be "Don't *you* know?" But there could be lightning flashes mingled with even louder thunder, then *"Yes—but do you?"*

Our forgiveness need is both simple and complex. It's simple to state but complex to work out and understand in the tangle of human relationships. And though readily available by the grace of God, it still requires an awareness of sin and a godly sorrow that leads to repentance.

As I pass along the halls of the church, I sometimes hear the bright sound of children's voices repeating, "Be ye kind one to another." They say it in chorus, and always in a kindly way. I smile and shake my head. I enjoy their simple, trusting faith. But I remember, as I go on to other things, that the rest of that children's memory verse says" . . . tenderhearted, forgiving one another, even as God for Christ's sake hath forgiven you" (Eph. 4:32,KJV).

It's easier said than done. The children will learn that in time.

Deliver Us from Evil

"Deliver us from evil," it says.

Deliverance implies peril; something we pray about, or need to pray about. It implies, too, that our fate rests in the hands of someone else. We're in a mess we can't get out of by ourselves, and someone must help us or we'll perish. This prayer is a prayer for rescue, as with someone locked in a cell and pacing, counting, waiting for footsteps and the turn of a key. Someone at someone's mercy.

Perhaps the flaw of most prayers is their lack of any desperateness. We pray as if nothing needs to change very much, as if things are pretty well under control. "But here's our list for today, Lord. Anyway, we wanted you to know we called!"

How far that is from a story Jesus told. A man goes to the Temple and is found beating on his chest and crying out "God, be merciful to me, a sinner" (Luke 18:13). If we found someone doing that in my church we'd probably call the mental health squad! The man in that story really felt his need of deliverance. And the thing that struck Jesus was the contrast between him and another man who was there at the same time and very nonchalant about the whole thing. Most of us are more like the second man.

Does this sound like I'm trying to make your life more distressing? Could be. In a world where evil abounds, as it does in ours, how can we not be distressed? Why, there's outrage in every morning's news! But we've learned to sip coffee and yawn as we read it. We read about some horribly destructive new weapon and say to the spouse, "Well, what'll they come up with next?" Or about people starving by hundreds of thousands in Africa—"That's a shame, isn't it?"

Where then *is* a prayer "deliver us from evil" said with moral earnestness? Could it be that the only way we get earnest is when it's in the singular, a "deliver *me*"? That isn't the way it is in the prayer the Lord gave. In fact, this is as good a place as any to count them up, those plurals in the Model Prayer. We ask bread for *us,* and forgiveness for *us,* and deliverance from the evil that threatens and tempts *us*. Every soul we pass on the road is a part of that *us*. Three times in the Lord's Prayer we're battered by that plural. And I don't think the Lord will take it kindly if we change them to the singular.

I've noticed in recent years a tendency for people to do just that; even in large gatherings where many people are praying together. Seven hundred people have their heads bowed, being led in prayer by this guy who's saying". . . and Lord Jesus, *I* thank you for what you've been doing in *my* life lately; you've blessed *me* with several new gifts of your Spirit and. . . ."

I've heard long prayers like that where every expression was *I, me,* and *my*. What about all those other people? What about the world beyond that room? What about the great *us* of earth? Maybe I'm being picky; if so, let the reader forgive me. But if the Model Prayer is really our model, let it be that. Even in our private prayers we should pray the *us* a lot. We should pray as with the company of others we belong to, and for them as well.[13]

Is deliverance from evil what we *really* want? From the evils of cancer and war and crooked politicians, it's likely we do. But what about our more personal and cherished evils? Our habit of judging others—do we really want deliverance from that? Our ungodly ambitions? Our pride of material possessions? Our secret lusts?

Those evils we cherish and protect. It's the evil of others we want deliverance from, not ours. Not our comfortable, home-made evils. "Deliver me from the evil of muggers and murderers—from their evil, O Lord. But leave my own alone! That I can handle. It isn't a problem."

Thus is the world composed of evildoers, each looking out for himself, each disapproving the evil found in others, but none concerned about changing his own.

So maybe a more useful version of the prayer would be something like this: "Lord, deliver us from evil, beginning with those evils of our own we haven't the slightest desire to be delivered from."[14] If you see it that way, it's not an easy prayer, and perhaps not a likely one. Let's hear a story:

> A man sat in the doorway of his home, smoking his pipe. He was poor and had many problems he thought about as he smoked in silence. He was out of work, had been for some while. There'd been promises of jobs, but times were hard, and nothing had worked out. And there'd been sickness with the kids, and there wasn't much to eat inside.
>
> Down the street someone was coming. The man recognized who, but in a dark sort of way. In front of his house, the visitor stopped. He had come to see him. It was business, he discovered. Had to do with money and how he could make a lot of it if things worked out. And no one had to know, he said so people inside couldn't hear. Not even his wife. So was he interested or not?
>
> Just then the man's wife showed up in the doorway. She glanced at the stranger and gave no sign. Then she said, "Here, hold the boy while I hang the clothes out back." The man took the boy and sat back down on the porch.
>
> The boy on his lap looked up and the man had two thoughts. He had one first, then the other. The first was about all that boy needed and couldn't have because of no money. The stranger was saying there could be money for that, and a lot of other things too. The man sighed a sigh as he thought about that. Then he looked back at the boy.
>
> The boy looked in his eyes. He didn't look any particular way, but the man had a sudden feeling about being the father of this boy. He sighed again. It was a heavier sigh this time. And then he told the stranger on his porch to leave and never come back.

That illustrates an aspect of what this part of the Lord's Prayer means. There are evils that tempt and tantalize us constantly, and we must pray to be strong against them. Often they come in guises. They have their arguments pro and con. So we must pray a lot.

"Deliver us from evil" means "deliver us from the bad." From our own badness and others', too. Either one can make us its victim. The fact that God doesn't hold you responsible for other people's badness is small comfort when you get beat up on! We need a prayer for a safer world, and that's what we have here, is it not?

> Deliver me, O Lord. Deliver me from cheats and crooks, especially as I grow older. Deliver me from flatterers and gossips and all loud talkers. Deliver me from evil people with attractive personalities I might fall under the spell of. Deliver me from sickoes who laugh at everything. And from all who carry deadly germs, or a deadly tongue. And from those with a quick-fix deal that sounds good but isn't.
>
> Deliver me, O Lord. Deliver me from years without a good night's sleep. From lessons learned too late. From mistakes you never get through paying for.
>
> Deliver me from radar traps when I have six points already. Deliver me from surgery on the morning after the guy's wife walked out. Deliver me from hilltops in a lightning storm. And from elevators with cables about to break.
>
> Deliver me, O Lord. Deliver me from the looks of people I've hurt. From angers I deserved. From innocence I misled. Deliver me from the death of pity in my soul, except of self. And from greed and the greedy, and the hell made by both. And from all hells, O God, whatever hells there are.[15]

Do you see now how much evil there is in the world? How much to be delivered from?

Soon after the home video games came out, our family bought one as a Christmas present. One of my early favorites involved invaders from space. The game begins with them coming to get you. And they're many, up there in the sky. If even one of them lands, you're dead in that instant. And they shoot at you as they come—three hits and you're dead as well.

But you, the lonely one against so many, aren't defenseless. You can move, and you can shoot. And there are shields you can hide behind to save you from the missiles raining down. Except that if you survive long, you anger that host of wickedness. And though you kill them every one, they'll come back at

you again, and much closer this time. Finally they're firing at
you almost point blank, and you with no shields to hide behind.

It's really terrifying, that moment. You can lose your three
lives in nothing flat, then the screen goes funny and reads out
the final score. I'm giving this as a modern parable of what the
final petition of the Model Prayer means:

> *My God, don't let me come to a place like that . . . in the
> game that matters.*

But it can happen. Remember how Jesus was "led up of the
Spirit into the wilderness to be tempted of the devil"(Matt. 4:1,
KJV). What went on out there was no game. It was a real and
vicious struggle. It was "How am I going to make it through
this?"

Might it be that there's where Christ first learned to pray
about deliverance from evil? If so, it comes not as something He
just thought up but as His own response to an actual situation
of life.

The Greek word translated *tempt* means literally to test. You
could say, of course, that testing only makes a thing stronger.
You put your biceps to the test on a chinning bar and make
them more powerful in the long run. Then is temptation a thing
to be sought and welcomed? Then why pray, "Do not bring us
to the test"?

Because there are tests we aren't ready for. There are tests
we don't need to mess with. There are tests no one can pass!

This, then, is a prayer of *conscious weakness*. It's the cry of
the poor in spirit. Let the guy at the gym beat a fist against his
midsection and dare you to hit him, he can take it. But if you
suppose your spirituality is that sturdy you should think real
hard. "Lord, we are able," those disciples bragged! But the
Master didn't think much of their spiritual readiness, or their
bragging.[16]

Are we really ready to drink from His cup and be baptized
with His baptism? Would we really follow Him to the garden?
If the soldiers come, what then? Would we stay by His side after

that, as they lead Him away, or follow afar off? Would we really go with Him all the way to the cross?

The prayer was given to help avoid some bad spots we have no business being in. And it's also for the rescue of those who must walk through dark valleys. We'll avoid some of those, but we won't avoid them all. We'll need that prayer.

Now I haven't told you everything about the Model Prayer because I don't know everything. I hope you've gotten some ideas and have done some thinking of your own. Perhaps the questions to follow will help as well. Also I hope you've gotten a feeling that it's OK to "mess with" the prayer. It was given for messing with. I mean we should feel free to take it piece by piece and *use* it as the teaching device it was meant to be.

In the next part we'll be doing a lot of "messing around" with prayer. Don't worry, the Lord understands our need. And we have much to learn. "We do not know how to pray as we ought, but . . ." (Rom. 8:26).[17]

Questions for Review and Discussion

1. Make a list of all the appropriate names you can think of (or find in this chapter) for what is usually called "The Lord's Prayer." Use your imagination!

2. Go back and pick out the five "movements" of the Model Prayer described in the beginning of the chapter. List these on paper. Then use them as the outline for a prayer of your own.

3. Can you think of an occasion when you've found yourself becoming the answer to your own prayer? If not, try to be more conscious of this in the future.

4. Discuss the author's point about Christianity being a "worldly" religion. Argue with it if you like. There's the other side, of course, but consider the point being made.

5. Reflect on the point that the Model Prayer implies a variety of threats. Try to remember prayers of your own in

threatened situations. In the next chapter, there'll be an exercise related to this.

6. Analyze your own praying in terms of its "asking" content. Do you have the "sweet tooth" spoken of in this chapter? What percentage of your prayer time is given to praise? confession? intercession? thanksgiving?

7. Expand on the thought of the practicality of prayer. List all the things prayer is good for. Imagine if people were charged for it by the hour, what would it be worth?

8. Discuss the author's point about the unselfishness of prayer. Is this too idealistic? If there were a selfishness index to measure your praying, what would it conclude?

9. Discuss the relationship of prayer and our efforts to evangelize. Then relate that to the freedom of people to live as they choose. What can you conclude about the part we play in the coming of the kingdom to others?

10. What do you suppose most people think of when they repeat "Thy kingdom come"? Now that you've read and thought about it through this chapter, will it mean something different for you?

11. Review the discussion in section four and try to imagine yourself in a situation of actual hunger. Then compose a longer prayer for daily bread.

12. Is "daily bread" talking about what we want or about what we need? What do you think of the discussion that suggests it calls for a modest life-style?

13. What have you asked of God lately that you would put in the category of daily bread? What are you thinking of asking?

14. Discuss the contrast between asking daily bread and asking for forgiveness of sins. Think of your own praying in these terms. How much time and effort is given to each aspect of the Model Prayer?

15. Discuss the illustration of Jimmy. Do you know a story like this? What are the requirements of "forgive us our sins" that have to be satisfied here?

16. Discuss how prayer is hindered by unforgiveness toward

others. Can you give examples of the joy and relief that comes through reconciliation?

17. What about the matter of praying in the plural as opposed to the singular? Does this make any difference? What is your own practice, and why?

18. When you pray "deliver us from evil," do you think of perils (like a nuclear war) or of personal temptation to sin? The author applies it to both types of situation. Is that valid, do you think?

19. The story of the tempted father in this chapter has more than one possible ending, of course. Imagine others, or take the story and write one yourself.

20. Was Jesus really tempted to sin, do you think? You can read Matthew's account beginning in 3:1. Discuss the author's connection of the temptation with the last petition of the Model Prayer.

Notes

1. As cited in Elton Trueblood, *The Lord's Prayers* (New York: Harper and Row, 1965), p. 53.

2. Ibid., p. 55.

3. George Buttrick, *The Interpreter's Bible*, VII (Nashville: Abingdon Press, 1951), p. 310.

4. Rudolph Otto, *The Idea of the Holy* (New York: Oxford University Press, 1958), p. 2.

5. Ibid., p. 13.

6. Ibid., p. 312.

7. William Barclay, *The Daily Study Bible*, Vol. I, *The Gospel of Matthew* (Philadelphia: The Westminster Press, 1958), p. 213.

8. E. Glenn Hinson, *The Reaffirmation of Prayer* (Nashville: Broadman Press, 1979), p. 134.

9. A rather biased and unsympathetic analysis, I know. But have you looked lately at all these books on the bookstore shelves and tried to imagine what the world would be like if everyone bought them and began living by them?

10. To give credit as best I can, I believe this point was expounded by William Temple and that I learned it through Elton Trueblood.

11. The term *sin* is used in this chapter because it seems a stronger and more explicit word in our language than others like "debts" or "trespasses." Also it's a word social usage hasn't corrupted as much as other Biblical words, like

"love" for example. "Sin" has been pretty much left alone, so it still has some clout.

12. This is as good a time as any to remark on one of the traits of my dialogue with you, the reader. To put it simply: I ask a lot of questions! I don't know how many good ones you'll find, but I do believe in the method. Jesus was its master. He absolutely never began with a person by telling what *he* thought about a thing. He asked questions that forced a person to think, and drew out of him his thoughts. That's a lot harder than being told the answer right from the start. It leaves you struggling and "hanging in the balance." But it's good for you. Be brave. Persevere!

13. You'll find this conviction of mine reflected in Part III—where I give you some prayers for everyday use. A few of those *are* in the singular, but most are in the plural. Some of them I've actually changed back and forth several times. I know the "I" seems more intimate and personal. I have tried to see both sides. But as the discussion above indicates, I feel rather bound to follow the scriptural pattern. Remember the disciples had asked Jesus to teach them to pray. This seems to me a matter which is central to the teaching. Well, I've made my point and will try not to harp on it any more! You can easily change all my prayers to the singular anyway!

14. I'm reminded of the saying I used to hear in country churches that "he's quit preachin' now and gone to meddlin'. "

15. This prayer, you may have noted, is in the *singular*. That's either an example of either inconsistency or flexibility. The reader can decide.

16. You can read that story in Matthew 20:20-28 or Mark 10:35-45. It may also be reflected in Luke 22:24-27.

17. Someone is saying to himself about now, "How can the chapter be over when we haven't even finished the prayer?" You know—"For thine is the kingdom, and the power," and so forth. That's a doxology, not one of the petitions. It's very nice and surely fitting to repeat. The prayer closes abruptly without it. So put it after this prayer, or *any* prayer.

Part II

Learning to Pray
——————Some Practical Help——————

You've been doing the easy part so far. You've been sitting in a chair and reading what someone else wrote about prayer. Easy!

Maybe you paid some attention to the questions for discussion at the end of the last chapter, or maybe you didn't. What about it? If you did work on those, and especially if you actually wrote things down, then you're good material for what's ahead.

If you didn't do that, then decision time has come. The following pages call for you to get actively involved in a prayer learning process.

If "prayer learning process" sounds funny to you, let's discuss it. Does it sound funny because you have a feeling prayer should just come naturally, like a baby growing up and learning to walk? If you're a child of God and have His Holy Spirit, all you have to do is just pray, right? And you feel uncomfortable with the idea of getting trained in how to pray?

I understand those feelings, but I have to argue with them. Nothing is really automatic about becoming a spiritually mature disciple. You learn to interpret Scripture, you learn stewardship, you learn ministry to people in need, you learn how to make an impact on society, you learn how to share your faith.

And you learn to pray. It isn't in a different category. If the disciples of Jesus could ask, "Lord, teach us to pray," why can't you? So do it, and let's quit wasting time and get started!

This may be the most valuable section of the book as far as lasting results are concerned. If you do it, that is. You'll be tempted to glance over it, tell yourself you might come back and do something with it later, then go on.

Stop! If you let that happen, you're done for! I mean, unless you get strongly motivated and jump right in now, you'll substitute intention for action and procrastinate forever. So I urge you to try. Please feel free, by the way, to duplicate the exercises for use by your family, class, or prayer group. And if you have a good experience, write and tell me. Also I'd appreciate any suggestions you come up with. My address is 801 University Boulevard, West, Silver Spring, Maryland 20901.

Now, most of these exercises call for you to write prayers down. Knowing you may not do that every day, and, in fact, may never have done it, let me speak about what it means.

In the wing of Christianity farthest from Anglicanism and Catholicism, there's often an entrenched prejudice against writing prayers and reading written ones. It feels so formal. It seems less spiritual. We hear echoes of Christ's blasting the Pharisees for their formalism and religion practiced for show on the street corners. We remember Paul's comment about a "form of godliness, but denying the power thereof" (2 Tim. 3:5, KJV).

I confess to some prejudice of my own when a Christian can only pray by pulling a piece of paper out of his pocket and reading it. A child of the Father should be able to speak with Him spontaneously, anytime, and anywhere. So if you too have that same prejudice, you can see I'm on your side—sort of.

On the other hand, leaving everything to spontaneity can lead to more vain repetitions than anything else! When you give your prayers no prior thought at all, you tend to say the same things over and over. You fall back on your store of previous thoughts and language. Phrases roll right off the tongue, but they're the same ones you used last week. You can almost stand aside and listen to it as a spectator.

You're acting much like a machine. The tape has been loaded, the "play" button pressed, the volume adjusted, and now we can all sit back and listen. In private prayer that's one thing, but in public prayer it surely falls short of being edifying to fellow believers over the long haul. They've heard it all before.

The ones with good memories know what you're about to say before you say it! I'm arguing for giving conscious thought to prayer, and writing is one of the best ways for doing that.

Think how the church has been blessed and nourished by the written prayers preserved in the Bible. There are hundreds of them, by the way. And how poor we'd be without them! Many are lengthy and quite detailed. What if there had been prejudice against writing down the words of a prayer when the Scripture was written? What if all we had preserved were some vague references like this: "Then Jonah cried unto the Lord from the belly of the whale. He said something about his distress, but no one remembers what!" Or this: "Then Jesus knelt down and prayed more earnestly. Only nobody caught what the words were!" I think you see my point.

The written prayers of the Bible were preserved for our use, our learning, our inspiration, and our guidance. In fact, the Holy Spirit Who moved men to write our Bible seemed to have a fondness for great prayers, for so many are included. So in reference to our prejudice against written prayers, I'm tempted to quote the lesson Peter leanred: "What God hath cleansed, call thou not common or unclean!"

As for the exercises coming up, you should expect to do some picking and choosing. Find one that looks easy and do it as a starter. Share what you work out with a friend or family member. Breaking down your reluctancc to talk about prayer is a victory in itself. Remember how Jesus spoke of agreeing in prayer with one or two others? If you'll follow that and enter some kind of prayer partnership as you do these exercises, you'll reap greater benefits.

Shall we get started?

Boldness at the Throne

Here's the idea

Isn't it true that there are limitations we impose on our praying? We pray for enough but not too much. We pray as if God is able to do something about our concerns, but nothing unreasonable! Well, the idea of this exercise is to free our minds of that limitation and pray as if whatever we ask can be granted. But do so wisely and in a way to please the Lord.

Verses to ponder

Let us then with confidence draw near to the throne of grace, that we may receive mercy and find grace to help in time of need (Heb. 4:16, RSV).

And this is the confidence which we have in him, that if we ask anything according to his will he hears us (1 John 5:14, RSV).

Now get started!

Write conversationally and as fully as you can. Skip any suggestions that don't seem to apply. Add whatever else the exercise seems to prompt. Then pray this prayer yourself, and share it with a friend.

O Lord, you know how small and few my prayers have often been. I've . . .

(Confess the limitations of your typical praying.)

I come boldly now to ask of You in more than just the usual way. For my own family first of all, that . . .

(Pray boldly for your loved ones.)

And for my church, I pray this prayer, O Lord:

(Ask for anything!)

And Lord, there are special needs among my friends I'd also like to trust to You . . .

(Remember, don't feel limited.)

The world is so great, and its problems so many! These, Lord, I lay before You now, and ask Your divine help:

(Pray as a world citizen.)

Help me, Lord, to believe in miracles, and to pray for miracles! I pray for . . .   and . . .   and . . .

and most of all for . . .

And now, Lord, don't let me go back to thinking small thoughts and asking small favors. Let me keep on in this boldness as I pray without ceasing. Amen.

Mine Enemies

Here's the idea

One sure and subtle barrier to effective prayer is a strained and unresolved relationship with another person. Jesus taught that the Father forgives our sins only as we forgive others. He also taught us to pray for our enemies. This exercise is to help us honestly face this important matter and bring it to God in prayer.

Verses to ponder

> You have heard that it was said, "You shall love your neighbor and hate your enemy." But I say to you, Love your enemies and pray for those who persecute you, so that you may be sons of your Father who is in heaven. . . . For if you love those who love you, what reward have you? Do not even the tax collectors do the same? (Matt. 5:43-46, RSV).

Now get started!

Write conversationally and as fully as you can. Skip any suggestions that don't seem to apply. Add whatever else the exercise seems to prompt. Then pray this prayer yourself, and share it with a friend.

This is hard, Lord! It brings me face to face with things I don't like to face. So help me, I pray, to . . .

(Continue to ask God's help.)

There are people I've hurt, Lord—whose forgiveness I need. They are
. . .   and . . .   and . . .

        because of . . .   and because of . . .

Would you help me to . . .

(Ask specifically for the help you need in these situations.)

There are people, Lord, who seem to have a problem with me, although
I don't know just why. But I'd like for things to be right with them. With
. . .   and . . .

        Would You give me Your help as I . . .

There are other people, Lord, I don't seem to like very well! Some I don't
even know, but I know their kind. I don't trust them, and surely couldn't
say I love them, as You do. They are . . .

        . . . and Lord with them, please . . .

And finally, Lord, let me think of my worst enemies in this world. Perhaps
. . .

        or maybe . . .   or?

        This is my prayer to You for them . . .

I know this prayer isn't enough by itself. There are things I need to do
toward these people. So help me, Lord, as I try to put into action the spirit
of this prayer. Amen.

A Prayer of Love

Here's the idea

The Scripture tells us that the "first and great commandment" is to love the Lord with all our heart and mind and soul and strength. But how often do we express our love for God in prayer? We say what we want, but not how we love—do we? So fashion and pray a prayer solely for that purpose. Think of it as a love letter to heaven!

Verses to ponder

> *I love the Lord, because he has heard my voice and my supplications. Because he inclined his ear to me, therefore I will call on him as long as I live (Ps. 116:1-2, RSV).*
>
> *He who does not love does not know God; for God is love (1 John 4:8, RSV).*

Now get started!

Write conversationally and as fully as you can. Skip any suggestions that don't seem to apply. Add whatever else the exercise seems to prompt. Then pray this prayer yourself, and share it with a friend.

I love You, Lord. I love you more than . . . and . . .

and even more than . . .

I love You, Lord! I love You because . . .
and because . . .

and because . . .

I love You, Lord. And I pray that my love for You may . . .
    and
        and . . .

I love You, Lord! And I want other people to know it, too! So help me, I pray, to . . .

I love You, Lord. And because I do, I promise You this:

(When you finish, close this prayer in your own way.)

For a Friend

Here's the idea

Jesus once said to Simon Peter, "I have prayed for you" (Luke 22:32). The idea of this exercise is to be able to say the same to some friend of yours, especially one who may be experiencing problems in life. You may even want to give your friend a copy of the prayer as a "love gift." After all, we exchange all sorts of things with our friends, but how often do we give the gift the Lord gave Peter?

Verses to ponder

Beloved, let us love one another; for love is of God, and he who loves is born of God and knows God. If any one says, "I love God," and hates his brother, he

is a liar; for he who does not love his brother whom
he has seen, cannot love God whom he has not seen.
And this commandment we have from him, that he
who loves God should love his brother also (1 John
4:7,20-21, RSV).

Now get started!

Write conversationally and as fully as you can. Skip any
suggestions that don't seem to apply. Add whatever else the
exercise seems to prompt. Then pray the prayer yourself, and,
as suggested earlier, share a copy with the friend it was meant
for.

Lord, You tell us to bear one another's burdens, and so fulfill the law of
Christ. I have a number of friends with special needs right now. They are
                who needs   and
who   needs   and   and   and

> (Briefly mention friends and their needs, all you can
> think of, but just listing them.)

I pray for each of them, Lord. But just now there's one of them in greater
need, and I want to devote a special prayer to him(her).

This is _____

> (Now pray especially for this friend as follows.)

Dear Lord, You know how I feel about . . . He(she) . . .

> (Express your relationship with this friend, your ap-
> preciation, and your Christian love.)

I think he(she) needs my prayers, especially just now, Lord. My prayer
is that . . . help him to . . . be with him as . . . bless him in his . . . heal
his . . .   and   and

(Make specific requests for this friend, as many as
you need to and can think of. Do not patronize, but
instead think of how you would wish to be prayed for
if you were in this person's situation. It might also
help to think of your friend as hearing or reading
your prayer as you write it.)

Lord, he's(she's) meant much to Your work. I thank You for him(her). And
I pray that in the future you'll help him(her) to . . .

(Ask whatever you feel might be most needed and
helpful in this person's service to God and others.)

May the Lord bless and keep you, [name]   . May He make
His face to shine upon you and be gracious unto you. May He lift up His
countenance upon you, and give you His peace, now and evermore.
Amen.

A Prayer of Distress

Here's the idea

There are situations in life that can literally render a person
"speechless." At the same time, one may also be rendered
"prayerless." There's a verse in 1 Peter where the author says:
"Beloved, do not be surprised at the fiery ordeal which comes
upon you to prove you, as though something strange were happening to you (4:12). No one is ever fully ready for a fiery ordeal,
but perhaps our thought about it in advance will help when and
if the time arrives. This exercise is given for that purpose.

Verses to ponder

> *The cords of death encompassed me, the torrents of perdition assailed me; the cords of Sheol entangled me, the snares of death confronted me. In my distress I called upon the Lord; to my God I cried for help (Ps. 18:4-6, RSV).*
>
> *The Lord is near to all who call upon him, to all who call upon him in truth (Ps. 145:18, RSV).*
>
> *Now my eyes will be open and my ears attentive to the prayer that is made in this place (2 Chron. 7:15, RSV).*

Now get started!

Write conversationally and as fully as you wish. Skip any suggestions that don't seem to apply. Add whatever else the exercise seems to prompt. This is not a prayer for now, of course, but spend some time in meditation on its meaning. And pray that should you face such a time you would do so in the strength of faith.

Instructions

The idea of this exercise is to imagine a dreaded moment, to put yourself in that situation to be extent you can, and then to compose a prayer which expresses your response. This shouldn't seem like a silly thing to do, but if it does, go on to some other exercise. Actually a psychologist would tell us we do this kind of thing quite often. We pass an automobile accident which had serious injuries, then later find ourselves "daydreaming" about such an accident happening to us. This is a normal response.

Now we want to attempt a faith response to such an imagined situation. Honesty is important here. It would be easy to construct a response according to what you think it should be, not how it would be. Remember that negative feelings have a place in prayer as well as positive ones. The Psalms make that very clear.

You probably should think of this prayer as something very

private. If you planned to share it with others it would increase the temptation to preach. So try to be totally honest in response to this situation.

A few weeks ago you had an unusual pain and ignored it at first. Then you decided you should see your doctor, which you did. He assured you it was probably nothing to worry about, but he should make some tests to be sure. One of those tests was an X-ray which showed a shadow where none belonged. A surgeon was called in and a biopsy taken. Two days later the lab report came back that it was, indeed, malignant. Your doctor has just come in and told you and has gone. You are alone in your hospital room. He told you some things about treatments and chances, but you couldn't pay much attention. You have cancer.

This could happen, of course. It does every day for someone. What will your prayer be like if it does? Imagine you have an uninterrupted half hour before anyone comes to your room.

For His Eyes Only

Here's the idea

Much of prayer concerns forgiveness, the forgiveness of sins. Whose sins? Ours, of course. But what sins? Ah! there's one of the great problems of our praying. We skip anything related to the confession of sins. We hope a general sentence asking the Lord to forgive us our trespasses will do. Yet more is surely required, especially in extended private prayer. We must bare our souls to God. He knows us, after all, better than we know ourselves. So why pretend to be better than we are? This exercise is designed to help us search the dark recesses of our lives so that we may really pray the prayer: "God be merciful to me a sinner" (Luke 18:13).

Verses to ponder

Seek the Lord while he may be found, call upon him while he is near; let the wicked forsake his way, and the unrighteous man his thoughts; let him return to the Lord, that he may have mercy on him, and to our God, for he will abundantly pardon (Isa. 55:6-7, RSV).

If my people who are called by my name humble themselves, and pray and seek my face, and turn from their wicked ways, then I will hear from heaven, and will forgive their sin and heal their land (2 Chron. 7:14, RSV).

Now get started!

Write conversationally and as fully as you wish. Skip any suggestions that don't seem to apply. Add whatever else the exercise seems to prompt. Then pray this prayer yourself, and share it with a friend.

Lord, I believe the worst thing I ever said was . . .
And my latest unkindness has been . . .
      or perhaps . . .   or . . .
The thing I desire, but shouldn't, which messes me up so often is
. . .
And my most constant, daily failing is . . .
      or it could be . . .   or . . .
The habit I most would like to change, Lord, is . . .
And my biggest sin of omission is . . .
      or perhaps? . . .   or . . .
The time I lately failed You most was . . . or . . .
Lord, the biggest regret of my life so far is . . .
And the person I most need a reconciliation with is . . .
And the sins today that I need Your forgiveness for are . . .
      and . . .   and . . .

*Have mercy on me, O God, according to thy stead-
fast love; according to thy abundant mercy blot out
my transgressions. Wash me thoroughly from my
iniquity, and cleanse me from my sin! (Ps. 51:1-2).*

(Read the remainder of Psalm 51, then close your prayer with
an appropriate plea for forgiveness.)

Thanks to the Father 5/18/87

Here's the idea

This is an exercise for a simple but comprehensive prayer of
thanksgiving. It prompts you as to an area of your life, and you
supply an expression of thanks to God. Don't feel limited by the
prompting, however. Attempt to count your blessings as of this
hour and give God the glory.

Verses to ponder

*Have no anxiety about anything, but in everything
by prayer and supplication with thanksgiving let
your requests be make known to God. And the peace
of God, which passes all understanding, will keep
your hearts and your minds in Christ Jesus (Phil.
4:6-7, RSV).*

Now get started!

Write conversationally. Perhaps you should attempt to in-
clude just one well-chosen sentence for each of the "prompts."
Skip any suggestions that don't seem to apply. Then pray this
prayer yourself, and share it with a friend.

Express your thanks to God for His blessings in each of the
following areas:
For life itself:
For prayers answered:
For His love and grace:
For salvation through Christ:
For your family and loved ones:
For friends:
For your health:
For material blessings:
For the church:
For the fellowship of Christian friends:
For your start in life and those who helped you:
For spiritual gifts:
For your country and freedom:
For the hope of heaven:
And for?
And, Lord, let the saying of my thanks be just a prelude to the living of
my thanks, as I serve You from day to day.

Amen.

A Diary of Private Prayer

Here's the idea

There's something of value in keeping a record on important
regular activities in our lives. How many different kinds of
records do you keep? The answer is likely more than you'd
guess offhand. Records are important for evaluating progress.
They're also motivating. They make us accountable. The idea
of this exercise is to design a form for keeping a record of our

personal prayer life, then fill it out as a sample of what an average week might look like. If this then seems like a workable idea for you, why not use what you produce as your own diary of private prayer. It may be a little hard to remember at first, but once it becomes routine, it should stimulate your prayer life greatly.

Now get started!

The form provided here is a blank one for you to use in designing your own diary page. It may be as simple or elaborate as you want to make it. Think, though, of something you will actually use. The impossible best can be the death of the possible good! To keep a record with one column and check each day if you remembered to pray on that day would be a large step in the right direction for a lot of Christians. Suggestions are given, however, for making your diary form more extensive.

The steps in this process are as follows: (1) Decide on what kinds of records you wish to keep in your diary each day. (2) Divide the form provided into that number of vertical columns. (3) Mark the columns as to the categories you selected. (4) Fill in this form as a sample, imagining what a typical week might look at if you kept this record conscientiously. (5) Then decide on your future use of this system, obtaining a notebook or other means of keeping the diary. Suggestions for types of entries are given, but use your own imagination.

PRAYER DIARY OF _____

       Week of   _____

place

headings >

_____

MONDAY

_____

TUESDAY

_____

WEDNESDAY

_____

THURSDAY

_____

FRIDAY

_____

SATURDAY

_____

SUNDAY

_____

  Comments _____

_____

_____

(Possible headings: time spent, people mentioned, needs expressed, Scriptures read, special concerns, results seen, feelings today, thanks given for, prayers offered, praise given, confession made)

See These Hands!

Here's the idea

Our praying often suffers from sameness. We pray in the same place, in the same way, at the same times, for the same things, with the same people—sameness. As with most things in life, variety helps. Have you ever noticed how you tend to sit in the same area of the church? You get used to it, and it seems comfortable. But try a change sometime and notice the difference. New people, a new perspective, and often your attention is greater. This exercise is to explore that possibility with our private prayer. In 1 Timothy, Paul mentions a little-known practice of praying while lifting holy hands. We will use that as a starting point. First, read the Scripture passage.

Verses to ponder

I desire then that in every place the men should pray, lifting holy hands without anger or quarreling; also that women should adorn themselves modestly and sensibly in seemly apparel . . . as befits women who profess religion (1 Tim. 2:8-10, RSV).

Now get started!

Consider the following list of unusual prayer practices. *Unusual* isn't used in a negative sense. It's unfortunate that it often has that connotation. Unusual simply means "not the usual," which may lead us to something quite worthwhile. See if you can imagine each practice as part of your own prayer life. If so, then consider how, and beginning when. Then think of other such styles of praying you might want to use.

LIFTING HOLY HANDS.   Not unknown, but surely an unusual practice. A kind of body language symbolizing fervor in petition to the Lord. Moses once did this as Israel fought a crucial battle, but his hands tired and had to be held by others. Imagine it as an occasional part of your own prayer life.

    1. Have I ever done this? when?
    2. What do I think about it?
    3. Do I want to try it? when?

KNEELING.   Practiced regularly by some Christians, but almost never by others. Those are the ones who ought to consider it.

    1. Have I ever done this? when?
    2. What do I think about it?
    3. Do I want to try it? when?

OUT ON A MOUNTAIN.   Jesus went often to special places for prayer: mountains, gardens, lakeshores. Have you ever prayed alone at night under the stars? during a snowfall? beside a mountain stream? in church at odd hours? This category refers to any unusual and stimulating location.

    1. Have I ever done this? when?
    2. What do I think about it?
    3. Do I want to try it? when?

WHILE DRIVING.   Some people use commuting time for extensive conversational prayer.

    1. Have I ever done this? when?
    2. What do I think about it?
    3. Do I want to try it? when?

EYES OPEN.   Actually the Bible doesn't tell us to close our eyes. What about prayer before an inspiring painting or work of art? Or overlooking a city, as Jesus did?

    1. Have I ever done this? when?
    2. What do I think about it?
    3. Do I want to try it? when?

CHANTING.   What if you repeated "Thank you, Lord" or "I love you,

Jesus" or "Fill me, Holy Spirit" for an extended period of time? Just those words, concentrating entirely on their meaning.

1. Have I ever done this? when?
2. What do I think about it?
3. Do I want to try it? when?

(These are but a few examples of what is possible. Let them stimulate you to think of others. Remember we all have a natural resistance to changing accustomed ways, and anything new seems funny at first. Be brave!)

For the Day Ahead

Here's the idea

We sleep as late as possible, get up, grab a bite, then rush off to work, where it's busy, busy, busy. Is that the way it is? If so, think. Wouldn't our days go better if we began them with prayer? And what should a "prayer for the day" consist of? No two days are alike, of course. But this exercise is to think of a typical day in our working lives and what a proper morning's prayer ought to consist of.

Verses to ponder

And in the morning, a great while before day, he rose and went out to a lonely place, and there he prayed. And Simon and those who were with him pursued him, and they found him and said to him, "Every one is searching for you." And he said to them, "Let us go on to the next towns, that I may preach

there also; for that is why I came out." And he went
throughout all Galilee, preaching in their syna-
gogues and casting out demons (Mark 1:35-39, RSV).

Now get started!

Write conversationally and as fully as you wish. Skip any
suggestions that don't seem to apply. Add whatever else the
exercise seems to prompt. Then pray this prayer yourself, and
share it with a friend.

Lord, as this day begins, I praise the greatness of your name! I give thanks
for life! And I pray that this day may mean . . .

(Express your hopes for this day.)

However busy I may be today, O Lord, help me remember to pray
at . . .   and . . .   or when . . .

(Express prayer times and occasions.)

Today, Lord, help me look for . . .

          and . . .   and . . .

(Speak of opportunities to share and practice your faith.)

Also help . . . today as he/she . . .

          and also . . .   and . . .

(Pray for friends who have special needs today.)

Give me patience and understanding in dealing with . . . today!

                    and with . . . too.

And please give me wisdom as I . . .   and . . .
and . . .

(Ask for help for special tasks today.)

Keep me from . . . (temptation)   and . . .   and
from . . .

And most of all, be so present in my life today, O Lord, that. . . . Amen.

Prayer for the Church

Here's the idea
The Bible tells us that Christ "loved the Church and gave himself for it." Since He himself said to His followers "As the Father has sent me, even so I send you" (John 20:21), we assume that every Christian is vitally concerned about the church. He is also concerned, of course, about His church. And His church needs prayer, daily prayer. With churches, as with individuals, it's surely true that we have not because we ask not. This exercise is to increase our prayer support of the body of Christ—His church, and His churches.

Verses to ponder
And so, from the day we heard . . . we have not ceased to pray for you, asking that you may be filled with the knowledge of his will in all spiritual wisdom and understanding (Col. 1:9, RSV).

*To this end we always pray for you, that our God
may make you worthy of his call, and may fulfill
every good resolve and work of faith by his power, so
that the name of our Lord Jesus may be glorified in
you, and you in him (2 Thess. 1:11-12, RSV).*

Now get started!

Write conversationally and as fully as you wish. Skip any
suggestions that don't seem to apply. Add whatever else the
exercise seems to prompt. Then pray this prayer yourself, and
share it with a friend.

I thank and praise you for our church, O Lord, especially for people like
. . .   who mean so much because . . .   and . . .   and
. . .   and . . .

(Give thanks for people and what they do.)

Please help our missionaries . . . in . . .
          and . . .   and . . .   and all missionaries.
Enlarge our vision, Lord, help us see . . .
          . . . and help us become . . .
Bless our pastor, we pray, that he may . . .   and . . .
          and let me . . . to help him . . .
Renew our worship of You, we pray, and especially help us to . . .
We face our problems just now. Especially be with us in . . . and give us
wisdom as we . . .
Lord, stir up those who've become inactive in serving You, especially
. . .   and . . .   and . . .
          . . . and if I can, help me to . . .
And as we serve our community and its needs, help us . . . especially
. . .
Renew Your church, O Lord, beginning with me!
     Make us . . .
     Rekindle our . . .

Lead us in . . .
And unite us as we . . .

In the Savior's name.
Amen.

A Model Prayer

Here's the idea

Jesus gave the Lord's Prayer in answer to a request from the twelve, "teach us to pray." Thus He gave it as a pattern or model. It was intended to be used, not simply said as is. The idea of this exercise is to take the Model Prayer, and your own understanding of what it means, and paraphrase it in your own words. You'll be interpreting the prayer, and also making a prayer of your own which closely follows the pattern it sets.

Verses to ponder

Our Father who art in heaven, Hallowed be thy name. Thy kingdom come. Thy will be done, on earth as it is in heaven. Give us this day our daily bread; and forgive us our debts, as we also have forgiven our debtors; and lead us not into temptation, but deliver us from evil. (For thine is the kingdom, and the power and the glory, for ever. Amen (Matt. 6:9-13).

Now get started!

You must do several things in preparation. First, review your understanding of the meaning of the Lord's Prayer. If you are unclear as to what Jesus meant by some part of it, you'll be at a loss. Second, decide if you want to make your model prayer in the first or second person. In Christ's prayer everything is *we, our, us,* but you might want to make yours *my, me, I.* Or you might want to write one of each! And third, you'll definitely need extra paper for multiple drafts.

Your own model prayer may be brief and concise like the original, or it could be much longer. Any of the petitions can easily be expanded with multiple sentences or even paragraphs.

Finally, this isn't an easy assignment! Don't expect to do it in a hurry. You may want to complete it over several working sessions. But the result should be well worth the effort.

Our Father, who art in heaven, Hallowed be thy name.

Thy kingdom come.

Thy will be done, in earth as it is in heaven.

Give us this day our daily bread.

And forgive us our debts, as we also have forgiven our debtors.

And lead us not into temptation, but deliver us from evil:

(Use doxology as is.)

For thine is the kingdom, and the power, and the glory, for ever. Amen.

Fruits of the Spirit

Here's the idea

Perhaps the finest statement of our goal for Christian maturity is Paul's in Galatians 5:22-23, where he describes the fruit of the Spirit. None of those fruits comes easily or automatically, and we never achieve them perfectly. We must pray about them, then pray some more; work at them, then work some more. This exercise is to construct a personal prayer for growth toward their ideal in our lives.

Verses to ponder

But the fruit of the Spirit is love, joy, peace, patience, kindness, goodness, faithfulness, gentleness, self-control (Gal. 5:22-23).

Now get started!

Write conversationally and as fully as you wish. Skip any suggestions that don't seem to apply. Add whatever else the exercise seems to prompt. Then pray this prayer yourself, and share it with a friend.

For love . . .

1. Pray for it.
2. Recall how Jesus exemplified it.
3. Confess your need of it.
4. Anticipate situations requiring it.
5. Ask God's help in achieving it.

For joy . . .

1. Pray for it.

2. Recall how Jesus exemplified it.
3. Confess your need of it.
4. Anticipate situations requiring it.
5. Ask God's help in achieving it.

For peace . . .

1. Pray for it.
2. Recall how Jesus exemplified it.
3. Confess your need of it.
4. Anticipate situations requiring it.
5. Ask God's help in achieving it.

For patience . . .

1. Pray for it.
2. Recall how Jesus exemplified it.
3. Confess your need of it.
4. Anticipate situations requiring it.
5. Ask God's help in achieving it.

For kindness . . .

1. Pray for it.
2. Recall how Jesus exemplified it.
3. Confess your need of it.
4. Anticipate situations requiring it.
5. Ask God's help in achieving it.

For goodness . . .

1. Pray for it.
2. Recall how Jesus exemplified it.
3. Confess your need of it.
4. Anticipate situations requiring it.
5. Ask God's help in achieving it.

For faithfulness . . .

1. Pray for it.
2. Recall how Jesus exemplified it.
3. Confess your need of it.
4. Anticipate situations requiring it.
5. Ask God's help in achieving it.

For gentleness . . .

1. Pray for it.

2. Recall how Jesus exemplified it.
3. Confess your need of it.
4. Anticipate situations requiring it.
5. Ask God's help in achieving it.
                              For self-control
1. Pray for it.
2. Recall how Jesus exemplified it.
3. Confess your need of it.
4. Anticipate situations requiring it.
5. Ask God's help in achieving it.
                              Amen!

Prayer Without Ceasing

Here's the idea

We're told to pray "constantly" or "without ceasing." It seems impossible! Of course, a stock answer has developed; we say it doesn't really mean without ceasing, it means to be "in a mood of prayer" all the time. No one knows quite what that means, but after it's said we all feel better and go home! Well, it surely means this: we should pray more than we do. What can help us?

Verses to ponder

Rejoice always, pray constantly, give thanks in all circumstances; for this is the will of God in Christ Jesus for you (1 Thess. 5:16-18, RSV).

Now get started!

Your purpose now is to brainstorm about a fuller prayer life. You will be given some suggestions which may prompt other ideas of your own. Evaluate the suggestions as to their usefulness for you, add others you come up with, then summarize what you would like to begin doing as an outgrowth of this exercise. Remember, it's better to propose one good thing and do it than dream about ten you'll never do!

————Questions, Ideas————   ————Notes, Response————

1. Do you have set times for prayer? Do you need more?

Are there times of the day you
   always have prayer?
What are some appropriate times
   as far as your schedule is
   concerned?
Missionary Luther Rice had set
   prayer times each day! Is that
   too much?
What do you suppose Paul did
   about this? Jesus?
What would you like to do?

2. Are there given situations which always prompt you to prayer?

Such as sitting down to eat?
Or before a big decision?
Or when you get good news of any
   kind?
Or bad news, of course.
Or following a conflict?
What others *should* prompt us to
   prayer?

3. Could physical reminders be of value?

Such as a Bible on your desk.
Or a painting on the wall.

Or something you carry in your
  pocket or wear.
Or some electronic something.
If not this, what?
   4. What about meetings for prayer with others?

Do you have a prayer partner?
Do you have a regular family
  prayer time?
Do you attend church prayer
  meetings?
Home prayer meetings?
What other such occasions could
  enrich your prayer life?
       Now make a summary of what you propose to do.

The Sharing of Faith

Here's the idea

The apostle Paul was always telling people to whom he wrote about his prayers for them. When he wrote to Philemon, he mentioned his prayer that the man would share his faith in Christ and that this would advance the cause of the kingdom. The sharing of our faith is vitally connected with prayer, both ours and others'. In this exercise we will explore this connection, both in responding to questions and in a prayer about the sharing of our own faith.

Verses to ponder
I thank my God always when I remember you in my prayers, . . . and I pray that the sharing of your faith

*may promote the knowledge of all the good that is
ours in Christ (Philem. 4,6, RSV).*

Now get started!

. First, answer the questions below. Then use the outline provided to write a prayer asking God's help as you share your
faith with others. Write conversationally and as fully as you
wish. Skip any suggestions that don't seem to apply. Add whatever else the exercise seems to prompt. Then pray this prayer
yourself.

Questions

(Complete these statements)
1. In my becoming a Christian, the persons who had the greatest influence were . . .
2. In my own Christian life, I have had a definite part in the
   conversion of . . .   and   and
3. I pray regularly that specific persons I know will find faith
   in Christ. Yes? No?
4. I participate in an organized Christian witness program.
   Yes? No?
5. I believe that prayer can make a difference in a person's
   accepting Christ. Yes? No?
6. I would like to have a greater influence for Christ in the lives
   of other people. Yes? No?

Prayer

Thank God for your own salvation through Christ.

Pray for greater personal concern for those who do not know
Him.

Pray for wisdom and guidance as you share your faith.

Pray for individuals you know right now.

Pray for boldness and courage.

Pray for the worldwide Christian witness.

Conclude in your own way.

To Whom We Pray

Here's the idea

We often focus on how we pray and what we pray for, but it may be even more important to consider whom we pray to. How do we feel about the God who hears our prayers? Do we come to Him in love or in fear, in faith or in doubt, or what? Actually, prayer itself can help in this, for there's a type of prayer which has as its main purpose the expression of our feelings to God. We call it *adoration*. Let us form a prayer which attempts to do this.

Verses to ponder

For thou, O Lord, art good and forgiving, abounding in steadfast love to all who call on thee. Give ear, O Lord, to my prayer; hearken to my cry of supplication (Ps. 86:5-6, RSV).

The Lord is near to all who call upon him, to all who call upon him in truth (Ps. 145:18, RSV).

If you then, who are evil, know how to give good gifts to your children, how much more will the heavenly Father give the Holy Spirit to those who ask him! (Luke 11:13, RSV).

Now get started!

Write conversationally and as fully as you wish. Skip any suggestions that don't seem to apply. Add whatever else the exercise seems to prompt. Then pray this prayer yourself, and share it with a friend.

Forgive me, Lord, if my prayers in the past have been about myself and my friends, and too little about you. In the future, help me to . . . and . . .   and . . .

Why do You care so much about me, Lord? It surely isn't because . . .   or because . . .   or . . .

It could only be because of . . .

Teach me your ways, O Lord! Let me learn more of . . . and . . . and . . .

Let me always come before You with more on my mind than just getting something from you. Let me think of Your . . . and . . .   and . . .

I thank You that You're always near me, Lord. Make me ever more conscious . . .   and . . .   and . . .

I . . . You, Lord, and . . . You. And I pray for . . .

In the Savior's name.
Amen.

This Day of Days

Here's the idea

This exercise follows a suggestion made by Saint Ignatius. The idea is to recall a special day of your past when things were good and right, and then pray as if it were that day again. Express what were then your feelings, give thanks for what were then your blessings, and ask for wisdom and spiritual help. This obviously requires thought and imagination, but it is worth the effort.

Verses to ponder

> At midday, O king, I saw on the way a light from heaven, brighter than the sun, shining round me and those who journeyed with me. And when we had all fallen to the ground, I heard a voice saying to me in the Hebrew language, "Saul, Saul, why do you persecute me? It hurts you to kick against the goads." And I said, "Who are you, Lord?" And the Lord said, "I am Jesus . . ." (Acts 26:13-15, RSV).

Now get started!

No promptings are suggested for this prayer. The first thing to do, obviously, is to decide on the time. Recall one where you were happy and secure, where God was real to you, and try to "be there" once more. Recall all you can about that time and your feelings there. Write your prayer from that time (write "I feel so fortunate now," not "I felt so fortunate then"). Express

things in your prayer you might not have expressed back then.
Ignatius suggested doing this often, visiting various stations of
your past. Perhaps you, too, will want to do it again. Good luck!

Bless This House

Here's the idea

The idea of this exercise is for a Christian family to collabo-
rate on a prayer asking God's blessing upon their home. It
should be "personalized" to reflect their own dreams and needs,
and their unique relationships. It will be best, of course, when
all members participate.

Verses to ponder

> *You shall therefore lay up these words of mine in*
> *your heart and in your soul; and you shall bind them*
> *as a sign upon your hand, and they shall be as front-*
> *lets between your eyes. And you shall teach them to*
> *your children, talking of them when you are sitting*
> *in your house, and when you are walking by the way,*
> *and when you lie down, and when you rise. And you*
> *shall write them upon the doorposts of your house*
> *and upon your gates, that your days and the days of*
> *your children may be multiplied in the land (Deut.*
> *11:18-21, RSV).*

Now get started!

Write conversationally and as fully as you wish. Skip any
suggestions that don't seem to apply. Add whatever else the

exercise seems to prompt. Then pray this prayer as a family, and save it for later revision. Try to see that each member makes some contribution to the final product.

Thank You for our home, O Lord. Thanks especially that we . . .
         and . . .   and . . .

Help us in our tasks of life, we pray. Help . . . with . . .   and
. . . with . . . (etc. for each family member)

And help us, Lord, in loving one another and in . . .
     We know we need . . .
     Give us patience in . . .
     Don't let us ever . . .

As we do things together, always . . .

Help us to be faithful to You, most of all, O Lord. Let us . . .
and . . .   and . . .

And let us remember our special friends and thank You for them, especially . . .   and . . .   and . . .

Each day we live, let us . . .

                Until at last we live forever with You.
                          Amen.

Depart in Peace

Here's the idea

This isn't for the faint-hearted or timid in their faith. The idea is to imagine the hour of your death and write a prayer as if you were there and had the opportunity to pray. The denial of death is constant human temptation. We live and pray as if we were to be here forever, but the fact is we aren't. If honestly done, this exercise can aid in your preparation for death. If it seems to hard, then go on to an other exercise. Perhaps you will return to it later.

Verses to ponder

> *Now there was a man in Jerusalem, whose name was Simeon, and this man was righteous and devout, looking for the consolation of Israel, and the Holy Spirit was upon him. And it had been revealed to him by the Holy Spirit that he should not see death before he had seen the Lord's Christ. . . . He took him up in his arms and blessed God and said, "Lord, now lettest thou thy servant depart in peace, according to thy word; for mine eyes have seen thy salvation" (Luke 2:25-31, RSV).*

Now get started!

You are on your own with this prayer—no prompting has been given. First spend a period of time in meditation and silence, attempting to get in touch with the feelings, fears, and anticipations of such an hour. There will be, for all of us, a last prayer. What would you want to pray in such a prayer?

Part III

In Spirit and in Truth
——Prayers for Every Day——

The idea of being a prayer merchant should make a person
stop dead in his tracks and think very hard. After all, who
knows his prayers are better than anyone else's? And what
does it say about the person if he *does* think they're better!

The fact remains, though, that people do need help. "Teach
us to pray" may not be on everyone's lips, but it's in everyone's
heart. It's buried deep perhaps, but it's there. We were all
created with a God-shaped void inside, and our hearts stay
restless until we do something to fill it. Man was made with a
capacity for communicating with his Maker, and never to use
that capacity is surely to frustrate something basic within us.

Was that theology? I suppose so. *Practical* theology, you
might call it. You see, you can come at theology in different
ways. Some people come at it from the intellectual slant. They
want to figure things out and satisfy their curiosity. They're
like the Athenians Paul met, whose daily delight was to hear
and learn some new thing, especially about religion.

But other souls take up theology in a less relaxed and casual
manner. They hunger and thirst. They come like the psalmist,
who likened his quest for God to the heated panting of a deer
in search of the water hole in summer. No intellectual curiosity
there. The most authentic prayers come from those who have
been literally driven to God. The problem there is that most
such prayers are lost and unpreserved for others' use. They are
trees fallen in the forest where no ears ever hear the sound.

The prayers included here are intended to reflect the mix
that is life. Some are happy, others sad. Some are casual, a few
profound. Some show great confidence, others reach out in

darkness. A few are angry. Read the Psalms and you'll find all those moods and more. In fact, one of our problems with praying is that we think we have to be in a religious mood or it won't work. We have to change clothes and put on our church face!

But read the prayers of the Bible and you'll find people came to God in all kinds of moods and circumstances. It's OK to appear at the throne of grace and say "Today I'm depressed, Lord" or "You don't seem near me right now." We have to come as we are, but *Come.* And to be natural before God as we do so. From Him are no secrets hid.

You'll notice each of the prayers that follow has a text and title. The title is to help you find it again if you ever want to. The more important thing, though, is the text. Each of these prayers follows closely the theme of a Scripture passage, a portion of which is included.

You may want to take your Bible and read more of this passage. And if you're using the prayers for family or group devotions, you may want to let one person read the lesson and someone else the prayer that follows. Think of the Bible reading as the Lord's speaking with us, and the prayer as our speaking with Him.

Also, try not to be concerned if some prayers get a little poetic. So does much of the Holy Bible. In fact, some of our modern problems with understanding the Bible may be the lack of poetry in our souls. We're used to thinking in figures and facts, not metaphors. Reading how the trees of the forest clap their hands fails to stir our hearts because it knits up our brows.

Some food products carry warning labels, and so do these prayers. The warning is this: saying the right words isn't nearly enough. The main thing is a spiritual attitude and a spiritual passion. Prayer is more than a literary exercise. In fact, some prayers need no words at all—a groan or a shout does very nicely. So use caution. These that follow may help—to that end were they given—but if so they must become yours. The laws of copyright permit it!

The Lord Is My Shepherd

The Lord is my shepherd, I shall not want; he makes me lie down in green pastures. He leads me beside still waters; he restores my soul. He leads me in paths of righteousness for his name's sake. Even though I walk through the valley of the shadow of death, I fear no evil; for thou art with me; thy rod and thy staff, they comfort me (Ps. 23:1-4, RSV).

Shepherd me, O Lord, for I've wandered far from You. The shadows were deep, almost like death, and there alone in that darkness I was afraid. Where were Your rod and staff to comfort me? I never felt them. But they must have been there, for I've been through the valley now.

Shepherd me, Lord. Even here where the pasture is green and pleasant. Even here beside waters that are still and cool. Even as I rest from the troubles of other valleys, be my shepherd. Without You I'm sure to wander again.

Don't let the ease of this day's rest make me forget the valleys of the past, I pray. Keep me from ever thinking I need no shepherd any more.

Lead me in the path I should follow, Lord. And give me the sense and the strength to follow it, all the days of my life.

In the Good Shepherd's name.
Amen.

The Dead Man

For I was hungry and you gave me no food, I was thirsty and you gave me no drink, I was a stranger and you did not welcome me, naked and you did not clothe me, sick and in prison and you did not visit me (Matt. 25:42-43, RSV).

That man I saw was so hopeless, Lord. His face set hard like anger, his eyes so vacant, as if he were dead already.

I suppose he is dead in a sense. Dead in the trespasses and sins that crowd his street. Dead to all churches, of course. Dead to the daddy he never knew. Dead to the hearing of good news or kindness.

What have I to do with such a man, O Lord? Whose job is it to worry over his poor lost soul? Can I feel good about the comfortable distance that separates his street from mine?

Why is it I see nothing but his face as I try to pray sometimes? As if his face has taken the place of Yours? As if it *is* Yours?

Oh please! Lord, let me do other work for You than having to love that man. Let me sing hymns in church and give money for the poor.

I who shake my head at the thought we are brothers. I who must be hindered in prayer until my soul repents.

Give me grace, I pray.
Amen.

A Secret Place

And when you pray, you must not be like the hypocrites; for they love to stand and pray in the synagogues and at the street corners, that they may be seen by men. Truly, I say to you, they have received their reward. But when you pray, go into your room and shut the door and pray to your Father who is in secret; and your Father who sees in secret will reward you (Matt. 6:5-6, RSV).

Lord, You know how hard it is to find the time and place to be alone. Noises everywhere, people everywhere, and it's easy to just live and think of little else. The world is so much with us!

And yet You call me to come to You in prayer, just me alone. In spite of the fact that I come often with others at the church.

It's easier with others, Lord. They don't know me as You do. With them it's easy to pretend, for all of us to pretend. With them I don't confess much. With them the prayer is almost automatic.

Out there the sound of words matters much. But in here, with You, in moments like this, the heart has to find its own language.

So I wait before You now and wonder: what do You think of me? How have I pleased You? How have I displeased You? Let Your Holy Spirit tell me, I pray.

Tell me what You'd have me do, this very day, for Your kingdom's sake. Amen.

Laborers for a Harvest

When he saw the crowds, he had compassion for them, because they were harassed and helpless, like sheep without a shepherd. Then he said to his disciples, "The harvest is plentiful, but the laborers are few; pray therefore the Lord of the harvest to send out laborers into his harvest" (Matt. 9:36-38, RSV).

Help us, O Lord, in knowing what time it is. There always seems to be time, but we know it's running out. Every day it runs out for people around us who know nothing about Your love. We pray to be more conscious of things like that.

Let us remember how Jesus went about preaching and calling people to repent. And let us remember He wants followers who do the same. It's like a harvest, and laborers are needed.

People are still harassed and helpless. Many have heard, but not with the heart; they've seen, but not with the eyes of faith.

We shrink from the call before us. You call us, the healed, to be Your healing agents in our cities and villages. But always we'd rather just celebrate Your healing of us, and let the rest take care of themselves. Forgive us, we pray.

The Master is here no longer. But He says to us, His own, "I send you out as I was sent; go and preach the good news of the Kingdom."

So into the harvest of this day's need, send us forth, we pray—moved by love, and strengthened by prayer. It's harvest-time, and we are Your laborers.

Amen.

The Danger of Living

*Finally, be strong in the Lord and in the strength
of his might. Put on the whole armor of God, that you
may be able to stand against the wiles of the devil.
For we are not contending against flesh and blood,
but against the principalities, against the powers,
against the world rulers of this present darkness,
against the spiritual hosts of wickedness in the heavenly
places (Eph. 6:10-12, RSV).*

We're so weak, Lord, and You're so strong. Help us never to
act as if it's the other way around.

The road we walk is one where danger waits, where armor
is the clothing of the wise. We know we mustn't walk as helpless
travelers, but as those who consider their steps.

What we'll face today, we don't know. But we know the devils
of this world are strong, and without your help we fall victim
to their wiles. So shield us, we pray, and give us the sword of
your Spirit. With that we'll do more than just survive.

Your Son, our Lord, was tempted in every way, yet without
sin. So must we be tempted. Strengthen us with His example
who loved You so dearly, and followed Your will so perfectly.

Lead us not into temptation, but deliver us from evil: For
thine is the kingdom, and the power, and the glory, for ever!

Amen.

Working Out Salvation

*Therefore, my beloved, as you have always obeyed,
so now, not only as in my presence but much more in
my absence, work out your own salvation with fear
and trembling; for God is at work in you, both to will
and to work for his good pleasure (Phil. 2:12-13,
RSV).*

Lord, You work out our salvation, then You turn right
around and tell us to work it out ourselves! It isn't easy to think
about that, but it surely will be good for us.

How often we've wanted this to be Your business, not ours.
We've tried to make our trust in You an excuse for ourselves.
We've asked your blessings on efforts that were far from our
best, as if it didn't matter very much. We've wanted the crown,
but not the cross.

Let us fear and tremble, Lord. Your mercy is great, but You
keep not your wrath forever. We must be about Your business.

Do help us work on love today, and joy, and peace. We know
we need patience and kindness, and soon will have a chance to
practice them. And goodness, faithfulness, gentleness, self-control—let those be our work for You today.

In the Master's name we pray.
Amen.

Wounded Healers

*Save me, O God! For the waters have come up to my
neck. I sink in deep mire, where there is no foothold;
I have come into deep waters, and the flood sweeps
over me. I am weary with my crying; my throat is
parched. My eyes grow dim with waiting for my God.
More in number than the hairs of my head are those
who hate me without cause (Ps. 69:1-4, RSV).*

Do You mind if we complain, O God? There are surely times
we want to. Our ears have heard bad news. Our eyes have seen
an ugly side of things. We've been perplexed, and often afraid.

Save us in such times, we pray. Save us from bitterness and
gloom. Don't let our troubles drive us from You; use them
instead to drive us to You. Let our crying be a crying unto You.
Let our waiting be a waiting for You. Let us know we never
have to face our problems alone.

We claim no other help but Yours. We need no other. And
even days when that seems but a wish, help us know it's the
only one we have.

We bring You our bruises now, to bind them up. Lay on us
Your hands of healing help, we pray. And so enable us that we,
the wounded, may then be healers of the hurts of others in
Your name.

Amen.

We on this Footstool

Thus says the Lord: "Heaven is my throne and the earth is my footstool; what is the house which you would build for me, and what is the place of my rest? All these things my hand has made, and so all these things are mine, says the Lord. But this is the man to whom I will look, he that is humble and contrite in spirit, and trembles at my word" (Isa. 66:1-2, RSV).

O God above, help us, we pray, to remember our place. So easily the world about us begins to seem bigger than it really is. It feels like it's ours, but isn't. We're only tenants here, renters and borrowers of things that aren't ours. We're short-term dwellers on the footstool of earth.

There's something else about it, too. The heaven You dwell in, Lord, is a place none attains except by Your will. Let us tremble at the thought, we pray. Let us be in awe of how these things work. Let us be humble, and not proud.

Forgive us when we've forgotten. And please think more of us, O Lord, than we've thought of You. Please love us more than we've loved You. And lead us, Lord, to love every glimpse of Your glory and might.

In our Savior's name.
Amen.

Deceptive Ease

The land of a rich man brought forth plentifully; and he thought to himself, "What shall I do, for I have nowhere to store my crops?" And he said, "I will do this: I will pull down my barns, and build larger ones; and there I will store all my grain and my goods. And I will say to my soul, Soul, you have ample goods laid up for many years; take your ease, eat, drink, be merry." But God said to him, "Fool! This night your soul is required of you; and the things you have prepared, whose will they be?" (Luke 12:16-20, RSV).

O Lord, it's You we depend on every day. And if the thought even starts to come in our heads that we don't, please help us get it out.

You know us well. There's no hiding from You the fact that often we've lived for the things of this world. We never joined the fool in saying "there is no God," but still our faith didn't make much difference in the way we lived. And we thought You understood.

You know if we were on a battlefield today, we'd call on You. Or in court. Or in surgery. In times like those we get more and more religious, and You must watch us and wonder.

So warn us, O Lord, this being such an ordinary seeming day, that it isn't at all. We need You every hour.

We know there's a last day coming. Let us know that today could even be it. And whether yes or no, help us use it for You. In the Savior's name we pray. Amen.

The Voice of God

*And when we had all fallen to the ground, I heard
a voice saying to me in the Hebrew language, "Saul,
Saul, why do you persecute me? It hurts you to kick
against the goads." And I said, "Who are you, Lord?"
And the Lord said, 'I am Jesus whom you are per-
secuting. But rise and stand upon your feet; for I have
appeared to you for this purpose, to appoint you to
serve and bear witness to the things in which you
have seen me and to those in which I will appear to
you' (Acts 26:14-16, RSV).*

We're always trying to be talkers, Lord, but maybe what we
need is to be better listeners. Especially with You. We talk, but
don't listen. It must seem that it takes a lot to get our attention.

Yet, You're always present in the world around us. And even
more in the world of the spirit within us.

The heavens and hills are telling Your glory, and the voice
of duty belongs to You. The beauty of stream and forest speaks
of You, and that urge to help someone is Your speaking in our
souls.

Let us know too, O Lord, that You often speak through other
people, even little children.

So let our ears be open, and our minds alert, to what You may
say to us, even this day.

In His name who was and is
Your living Word.
Amen.

Good Treatment

*A man was going down from Jerusalem to Jericho,
and he fell among robbers, who stripped him and
beat him, and departed, leaving him half dead. Now
by chance a priest was going down that road; and
when he saw him he passed by on the other side. So
likewise a Levite, when he came to the place and saw
him, passed by on the other side. But a Samaritan, as
he journeyed, came to where he was; and when he saw
him, he had compassion, and went to him and bound
up his wounds (Luke 10:30-34, RSV).*

Let people smile when I pass them today, for a smile is pleasant, Lord. And let them listen when I speak, for that's always appreciated. And today if there are some I've wronged, who hold their grudges and keep their distance—if You can, O Lord, help them forgive. That would be so nice!

And may I hear today a good word from someone I didn't expect. And may I get some good advice. And for heaven's sake don't let anyone cut in line in front of me, You know how that makes me mad. And let no one honk his car horn behind me today, that can get me all upset, and . . . *and now I see that something is wrong with this prayer, and maybe with my prayers.*

Forgive me this prayer, I pray. Forgive me of concerns for myself that ignore the needs of others. Let me pray instead that as I would that people should do to me, I shall do toward them, beginning this day. Amen.

Going Forward

Not that I have already obtained this or am already perfect; but I press on to make it my own, because Christ Jesus has made me his own. Brethren, I do not consider that I have made it my own; but one thing I do, forgetting what lies behind and straining forward to what lies ahead, I press on toward the goal for the prize of the upward call of God in Christ Jesus (Phil. 3:12-14, RSV).

Right now we're here at this dividing line, O Lord. We're here where the past ends and the future begins. We're here where the past can never be changed. And we pray to know what to do about that.

Save us from living with vain regrets. Save us from nursing whatever hurts we've suffered. Help us take life as given us this day and do our best with it. Let us tie a knot in the rope of days and determine not to slip back from here.

Forgive, O Lord, our jealous discontents. Our notice of those who have more wealth. Our worries over things imagined. Our small complaints against one another. Help us to really put such things behind us.

We thank You, Lord, that You're ever patient with us. We thank You that You never turn away from any honest prayer. For that we love and praise You.

In Jesus' name.
Amen.

The Father's Love

See what love the Father has given us, that we should be called children of God; and so we are. The reason why the world does not know us is that it did not know him. Beloved, we are God's children now; it does not yet appear what we shall be, but we know that when he appears we shall be like him, for we shall see him as he is. And every one who thus hopes in him purifies himself as he is pure (1 John 3:1-3, RSV).

Our Father in heaven, how often we need to be reminded that You love us. We are children You love, and You will do us good as often as You can. We hear such things said, but help them be a more constant awareness that fills our hearts and minds.

Let this deliver us from fears that nag, and even from the fear of You we have at times. We aren't strangers, and we shouldn't live as if we were. We pray to live in the confidence and liberty of those who know You and are known by You.

There's no fear in love, You tell us. Your love is perfect love; it casts out fear. So hear today our prayer that love may be stronger in us day by day.

Ruler of winds and waves, don't let the sea of troubles overwhelm us. Let us hear You say, "Fear not." Speak peace, and let our souls obey.

Amen.

Few Days

Man that is born of a woman is of few days, and full of trouble. He comes forth like a flower, and withers; he flees like a shadow, and continues not. Since his days are determined, and the number of his months is with thee, and thou has appointed his bounds that he cannot pass, look away from him, and desist, that he may enjoy, like a hireling, his day (Job 14:1-2,5-6, RSV).

You know, Lord, how we shrink from any reminder that our days here are few. We dread thinking today is one less day, so usually we don't. We act as if we can save life up like pennies in a jar, but deep inside we know that won't work. Our days aren't for saving but for using.

Pray tell us what to do about this. Should we get off our knees right now and run to right some wrong? Or should we stay here this livelong day, refusing to go until You bless us?

Our dilemma is, we don't know which to do. And the truth is, we likely will do neither. Some other day, we'll say, and then forget.

But somewhere, somehow, while days remain, do give us such a day. A day for setting things straight with You and the people we've lived among.

Just maybe we can get it started after all. Take our hand, we pray, and lead us to it.

Amen.

Pieces of Silver

*Then one of the twelve, who was called Judas Is-
cariot, went to the chief priests and said, "What will
you give me if I deliver him to you?" And they paid
him thirty pieces of silver. And from that moment he
sought an opportunity to betray him (Matt. 26:14-16,
RSV).*

Lord, there are many wicked things to do in this world. But
surely none is greater than to betray a friend. We say it's a
terrible thing, but still there comes a time to join those disciples
in that upper room and ask if it could be us.

For we're called Your friends, and haven't always acted like
it. We've had our love of money instead of You. We've had our
jealousy of those more prosperous. We've nursed our pride in
this or that as if it were our doing, not Yours. We've even
spoken evil of some you call our brothers and sisters, thinking
it bettered our reputations.

We don't wear the name of Judas, but we have this to think
about. Help us, we pray, in those small betrayals of our Savior
that come so easily: His name unspoken, His house neglected,
His example unremembered.

Let us take no man's silver for that, we pray.

Amen, and amen.

Father, Forgive Them

Two others also, who were criminals, were led away to be put to death with him. And when they came to the place which is called The Skull, there they crucified him, and the criminals, one on the right and one on the left. And Jesus said, "Father, forgive them; for they know not what they do." And they cast lots to divide his garments (Luke 23:32-34, RSV).

O Father of our Lord Jesus Christ, we marvel at His cross. We see there how He forgave, and we stand amazed. So it's our greatest hope, but also our greatest lesson. And we know we must learn it better.

Help us think of that, we pray, as we hold our grudges against one another. As we show no kindness, and give no mercy. We who've suffered the print of no nails or the striking of blows in our face, still strike out at one another. We all deserve a cross of our own, every one.

So our prayer is a sinner's prayer, but we thank You it can be. We thank You for the blood of Jesus Christ that cleanses us from all sin.

To Him we pray: "Forgive us, for we know not what we do."

Amen.

Come and See, Go and Tell

Remember how he told you, while he was still in Galilee, that the Son of man must be delivered into the hands of sinful men, and be crucified, and on the third day rise. And they remembered his words, and returning from the tomb they told all this to the eleven and to all the rest. Now it was Mary Magdalene and Joanna and Mary the mother of James and the other women with them who told this to the apostles; but these words seemed to them an idle tale, and they did not believe them (Luke 24:6-11, RSV).

You've set the issues plainly before us, O God. Death or life, failure or promise, idle tale or eternal truth.

Ah! the world is so filled with idle tales—it surely needs no other! And some think we're trying to add one more, and they even call us fools for believing it. But if we must be called fools, O God, let it be for Christ, we pray!

The cross is easy to believe—earth's roadways have been lined with them. But take us to His tomb, and let our Easter faith be kindled again.

Death was beaten there—thanks be to You, O God. Hope was given, eternal life was offered to all who believe—thanks be to You, O God.

And now, having come and seen, let us go and tell others, too. And bless us in the telling.

In His name we pray.
Amen.

Gathered in His Name

Again I say to you, if two of you agree on earth about anything they ask, it will be done for them by my Father in heaven. For where two or three are gathered in my name, there am I in the midst of them (Matt. 18:19-20, RSV).

O God, to be with a friend in Christ is to be very close to You. We feel Your presence in the presence of friends, and we feel your absence in their absence. And that's what You intended.

How good to join hands around a table of food! How good to join in covenant one with another, and in prayer. Surely you're pleased with such things. So help us, we pray, in our reaching out to others.

We have "brothering" and "sistering" to do, if two or three are to gather in Your name. We must overcome the distance we keep. We must lay aside small jealousies. We must love as You love us.

Forgive us if we're slow about this, Lord. It's surely easier and safer just to stay apart. But prod us if You need to, and bring us together. We will praise You for it.

Amen.

The Lesson of Trust

Therefore I tell you, do not be anxious about your life, what you shall eat or what you shall drink, nor about your body, what you shall put on. Is not life more than food, and the body more than clothing? Look at the birds of the air: they neither sow nor reap nor gather into barns, and yet your heavenly Father feeds them (Matt. 6:25-26, RSV).

Lord, it's hard to trust You as we should, not just because we have our fears, but because we're always trying to get ahead of one another. We try to set our minds on heavenly things, but we keep on competing with one another in earthly things.

We confess we're no people of simple wants, as we ought to be. There's much we still want, and when we get that there's always something more.

Even our prayers to You have been a tool of our wanting at times.

Do help us be satisfied with less, we pray. Less that serves the flesh, so we can be richer in things of the spirit, less goods laid up on earth, and more in heaven with You.

O Maker of the birds, help us see today how little they have, but how sweetly they sing, and how freely they fly. And You take care of them. Let theirs be our trust in You, we pray.

Amen.

Cups of Water

He who receives a prophet because he is a prophet shall receive a prophet's reward, and he who receives a righteous man because he is a righteous man shall receive a righteous man's reward. And whoever gives to one of these little ones even a cup of cold water because he is a disciple, truly, I say to you, he shall not lose his reward (Matt. 10:41-42, RSV).

How often we fail, O God, for lack of a kind and generous spirit. So much has its price. So often we're tempted to measure a thing as to how it may benefit us. It seems no one holds out his hand to give freely.

And yet You give freely to us—we live on Your bounty. And You teach us to do so with one another. So we need Your forgiveness, and we need Your help.

In this selfish and grasping world, we must strive to become a generous people. We must share of our means, of our time, of our love and care, and even the simplest of gifts—cups of water given in Your name.

How easy that sounds when there's enough. But what will we do when it means giving something precious to us? As if water were scarce, and we were thirsty, too, what then? What if a cup was all we had?

Help us think well on that, Lord. And help us decide as You decided when You gave for us Your only begotten Son. In His name we pray.

Amen.

In Everything Give Thanks

And let the peace of Christ rule in your hearts, to which indeed you were called in the one body. And be thankful. Let the word of Christ dwell in you richly, teach and admonish one another in all wisdom, and sing psalms and hymns and spiritual songs with thankfulness in your hearts to God. And whatever you do, in word or deed, do everything in the name of the Lord Jesus, giving thanks to God the Father through him (Col. 3:15-17, RSV).

We thank You, Lord, for everything that will sustain and bless our lives today, which often we take so thoughtlessly. Again, we say thanks.

And thanks for the help of others we'll be receiving. Even for little things like quiet glances and simple understanding, which mean so much. And, of course, for the labors of those who serve us on Your behalf. We give You thanks, O God.

And thank You for Christ Jesus, our Savior and Lord. Thank You that He calls us friends, not servants. His words are our hope, His example our daily inspiration. Thanks be for Him.

And thanks for our health, whatever it may be, and for the breath of life within us now, enabling our prayer before Your throne of grace. We pray, accept our thanks.

And forgive, O Lord, our way of thinking more about what we lack than about what we have. Give us daily gratitude for all Your hand provides.

Amen.

By a Cloud Surrounded

Therefore, since we are surrounded by so great a cloud of witnesses, let us also lay aside every weight, and sin which clings so closely, and let us run with perseverance the race that is set before us (Heb. 12:1, RSV).

Whatever we are today, O Lord, we are because of those who helped us in the past. Our parents who gave us birth, who raised us, and bore with our foolishness, who told us first of Jesus. We thank You for them today.

And for teachers and friends of early life, some forgotten now and nameless, who filled up days with the wonder of learning new things. We thank You for them.

For the preachers, too. Those by whom we came to know You better. We thank You for them today.

For everyone whose example raised our sights in life, whose pat on the back kept up our spirits in hours of stress, we thank You, O God.

And now, for those around us here, who look our way for help, whose example we are now—we pray for them, as part of that cloud of witness by which we live surrounded.

To them, to all, and to You above all, O God, we pray to give our best.

In Jesus' name.
Amen.

A Prayer for the Church

He said to them, "But who do you say that I am?"
Simon Peter replied, "You are the Christ, the Son of
the living God." And Jesus answered him, "Blessed
are you, Simon Barjona! For flesh and blood has not
revealed this to you, but my Father who is in heaven.
And I tell you, you are Peter, and on this rock I will
build my church, and the powers of death shall not
prevail against it" (Matt. 16:15-18, RSV).

How poor we would be, O Lord, without the church! The little church whose members we know so well, and the great church whose members are known but to You. We give thanks for them both.

For fellowship we share, and the hymns of faith that live in our hearts. For preaching and the preachers, and for sharing tears with those who weep, and embracing with those that rejoice.

For study that makes Your word a light to our path, and for helping the poor and homeless in the name of Christ. For leading others to call on Your name and walk Your way with us.

For that table where the supper of our Lord is spread, and for laying to rest those who've ceased from their earthly labor. For these and all such blessings, we give You thanks, O God. Truly they come from Your hand.

And now as Christ did love the church and give Himself for it, let us who honor Him go and do likewise.

Amen.

A Difference Shown

You are the light of the world. A city set on a hill
cannot be hid. Nor do men light a lamp and put it
under a bushel, but on a stand, and it gives light to
all in the house. Let your light so shine before men,
that they may see your good works and give glory to
your Father who is in heaven (Matt. 5:14-16, RSV).

Lord, we don't want to leave any doubt about whose side we're on. We know how much difference there is between Your side and the other. And we know You want that difference seen in us.

So help us at the crossroads of love and hatred, calmness and fear, truth and falsehood, self-giving and self-serving. And all the other places where good and evil intersect in our lives, and we must go one way or another.

Remind us too that it's the reality known to You and not the appearance of a thing that matters most. Even if we have to look false to every man, we must be true to You. So don't let us have the kind of religion that makes a parade all the time, but cares none for what You see and think.

Strengthen us for confessing Your name before men this very day, as someday You'll do with ours before the angels of heaven.

What a day that will be!
Amen.

Another Try

And when he had ceased speaking, he said to Simon, "Put out into the deep and let down your nets for a catch." And Simon answered, "Master, we toiled all night and took nothing! But at your word I will let down the nets." And when they had done this, they enclosed a great shoal of fish; and as their nets were breaking, they beckoned to their partners in the other boat to come and help them (Luke 5:4-7, RSV).

O Lord, we've known our times of toiling through a night and seeming no better for it. We've even toiled in Your service and seen no results. We've dreamed our dreams of full nets and still found them empty. We've been tired and discouraged, as You know well.

In times like those, it's hard to go right back out and try again. Where do we get the faith to believe it may be different? Where, if not from You, O God?

Give us then, as we need it, the hope of new possibilities, we pray. Even when we've failed at something once, let us be willing to try again. If we've said a thing unwisely, let us go and say it better. And don't let us ever give up on anyone, Lord, for You don't.

Keep us from being weary in our well-doing. Make Your Holy Spirit our Comforter in every stressful hour. And, at Your bidding, let us ever be ready to try, or try again.

In the Master's name. Amen.

Not Hearers Only

But be doers of the word, and not hearers only, deceiving yourselves. For if any one is a hearer of the word and not a doer, he is like a man who observes his natural face in a mirror; for he observes himself and goes away and at once forgets what he was like. But he who looks into the perfect law, the law of liberty, and perseveres, being no hearer that forgets but a doer that acts, he shall be blessed in his doing (Jas. 1:22-25, RSV).

We do confess, O God, that often we've tried to let the hearing of Your Word be a substitute for doing what it commands. It's surely good to study and learn, but a time comes to put it into action, and we pray You'll help us move quickly to that.

We don't want to be of those who sit and enjoy pleasant discussions in Your name while refusing to help people in need. They love in word, but not in deed and in truth. Help us always beware, lest that be our way, too.

Give us glimpses in the mirror of truth, Lord. Let us see things as they are, then get busy on what needs doing. If we're to make mistakes, which of course we are, don't let them be in hesitating to act, we pray.

As your Word became flesh and blood in Jesus Christ, living and active in the life of earth, so let it be in us, as we follow Him. We pray in His name.

Amen.

To the End of the Earth

But you shall receive power when the Holy Spirit has come upon you; and you shall be my witnesses in Jerusalem and in all Judea and Samaria and to the end of the earth (Acts 1:8).

We pray for Jerusalem, Lord. It's our home, our city, our own small corner of the wideness of earth. And we're here for something, or someone, or perhaps many someones who live about us with no knowledge of You. We're called to be your witnesses, beginning with them. Help us, we pray.

We pray for Judea, Lord. It's our land, our country. We pledge it our allegiance, but always remembering we have other allegiances too. Help us here, we pray.

We pray for Samaria, Lord. The neighbor lands about us, and even the Samaritans among us. Sometimes we find it hard to live with them, to understand and appreciate them. But our Lord went through Samaria, and we must, too. Direct us as we go.

We pray for peoples to the ends of the earth, Lord. North and south and east and west, its uttermost parts. All for whom Christ died. All of whom His Great Commission speaks. Reach out to them through us, with the message of salvation we preach in His name.

Amen.

Jesus Wept

Then Mary, when she came where Jesus was and saw him, fell at his feet, saying to him, "Lord, if you had been here, my brother would not have died." When Jesus saw her weeping, and the Jews who came with her also weeping, he was deeply moved in spirit and troubled; and he said, "Where have you laid him?" They said to him, "Lord, come and see." Jesus wept. So the Jews said, "See how he loved him!" (John 11:32-36, RSV).

You tell us, Lord, to weep with those who weep. So there's weeping to be done every day of our lives, if we only knew it. The mournful are all about us.

Some are lonely, some have children in trouble. Some have lost jobs, or health, or faith in themselves. Others sit in prison cells. Some have been hurt by the cruelty of this world, and some feel guilty, but can't find forgiveness.

The earth is soaked from crust to center with such tears. And even our Lord added to their number: weeping for friends, weeping over cities, weeping His tears in Gethsemane, weeping for us perhaps.

He was called a Man of sorrows. Help us, we pray, in finding out what that means, and what it should mean for us. For in being His follower we must know something of His sorrow. Strengthen His Spirit in us for the facing of such hours, we pray in His name.

Amen.

Every Need Supplied

*I have received full payment, and more; I am filled,
having received from Epaphroditus the gifts you sent,
a fragrant offering, a sacrifice acceptable and pleas-
ing to God. And my God will supply every need of
yours according to his riches in glory in Christ Jesus
(Phil. 4:18-19, RSV).*

You alone, Lord, know exactly what we need. You know it
better than we do. We seem to want so much, and surely don't
need it all. So keep us from wanting too much, we pray, and let
us be glad enough when we have what we need.

We want to be rich, or we want to be famous. We want to get
the best of someone who did us wrong. We want long life, or
constant peace, or the ease to stay in bed all day. We want
others to love and admire us. And the list goes on.

People everywhere are seeking those things. But give us a
better wisdom, we pray. Let us trust in You, Lord, not only to
supply what we need but to know what it is.

Let us not even try to say. Let us put our faith in the promise
of Your love, and in it trust, and wait. Let us curb our wanting,
and strive for different goals. Let us follow Your way, and know
that whatever comes of it will be the best.

Amen.

His Work, and Ours

The Lord sets the prisoners free; the Lord opens the eyes of the blind. The Lord lifts up those who are bowed down; the Lord loves the righteous. The Lord watches over the sojourners, he upholds the widow and the fatherless; but the way of the wicked he brings to ruin (Ps. 146:7-9, RSV).

O Lord, help us find out what You're doing in our world so we can join You in it. We want to work Your works. We want to be about your business.

The things we see You doing are so different from the ways of men. You give and ask nothing in return. You lift up those bowed down. You join the widowed and the fatherless in their plight. You set the prisoners free. You are known, most of all, for Your works of love.

We pray it may be the same with us. Don't let us be content with talk of love, or songs, or anything other than the doing of what it means in actual living.

Even now, Lord, even in this prayerful moment, turn our thoughts to when and how Your likeness may be better seen in us. Make us ready to give something away. For in such giving we find our greatest joy.

Let us go now and prove it!
Amen.

Standing Before the Throne

Then I saw a great white throne and him who sat upon it; from his presence earth and sky fled away, and no place was found for them. And I saw the dead, great and small, standing before the throne, and books were opened. Also another book was opened, which is the book of life. And the dead were judged by what was written in the books (Rev. 20:11-12, RSV).

There are places, Lord, we'd like never to have to go, and surely your judgment is one of them. Earth and sky flee away from there, and we would too, if only we could.

There are books, Lord, we'd like never to see opened. They hold the chapters of our lives, and there are pages there we wish we could change, but can't, of course.

Sober us, O Lord. Sober us with knowing that judgment has already started, that we live under it every day. What we say, we say unto You. What we do, we do unto You. Even what we call our private thoughts are spread open before You.

But still, amid all these sobering realities, gladden us in knowing Your judgment isn't that of men. And You wish us well, not harm. You love us as Your own dear children, even when we stray from Your will.

So don't let us live in dread, but rather let us labor to put on the page of today a reasonable service.

Amen.

With Those Who Differ

John answered, "Master, we saw a man casting out demons in your name, and we forbade him, because he does not follow with us." But Jesus said to him, "Do not forbid him; for he that is not against you is for you" (Luke 9:49-50, RSV).

Lord, You know how we sometimes love a good fight! And how we often try to call it Your fight, when it's really ours. We fail to do Your will for lack of a broad and generous spirit. We criticize what we don't understand; we avoid people whose language sounds a little strange.

Help us somehow to learn that You haven't made us judges of other people! Help us to remember that the last word is always Yours! And don't let us want or need the control of others' lives. Help us take a towel and wash feet instead.

Preach to us, Lord! Preach the lesson that there are always those whose service is better than ours, that we're no favorites. Humble us, we pray.

Guard our lips from speaking rashly, and our hearts from being high and mighty. Guard our spirits from all that's mean and low as we deal with those who differ. And if doing that should force us to go a mile, help us still be ready to keep on and go two.

In the Master's name.
Amen.

Bearing Burdens

Brethren, if a man is overtaken in any trespass, you who are spiritual should restore him in a spirit of gentleness. Look to yourself, lest you too be tempted. Bear one another's burdens, and so fulfill the law of Christ (Gal. 6:1-2, RSV).

O God of ever-present help, don't let the weight of our own load be the only burden we ever bear. We surely need Your help with it, but help us think of others, too. Show us how we sometimes better ourselves by forgetting ourselves.

And Lord, forgive us when we've added to others' burdens. Forgive our censure and blame we've piled on their shoulders. Forgive the times we delighted in someone else's misery. Forgive the hardness of heart that's let us pass by on the other side when someone needs help.

Gentle us, Lord. Touch us with feelings of others' infirmities. Help us know their grief could have been ours, and might be still. Don't let us be proud. Just help us remember how Jesus did.

In His name we pray.
Amen.

In Temptation's Hour

The devil took him to a very high mountain, and showed him all the kingdoms of the world and the glory of them; and he said to him, "All these I will give, if you will fall down and worship me." Then Jesus said to him, "Begone, Satan! for it is written, 'You shall worship the Lord your God and him only shall you serve.'" Then the devil left him, and behold, angels came and ministered to him (Matt. 4:8-11, RSV).

Help us, O Lord, for temptation is all about. We've seen it from the mountains of our ambition, and desired it. We've even listened to the voice that whispered how to get that wealth of earth, and get it cheap. And we've thought of doing it.

Strengthen us against that voice, we pray. Don't let us bow down to it, ever. Don't let us worship the wealth it speaks of. Whatever the offer we hear, help us say "Begone!" as Jesus did.

Help us see the more important thing: that the world passes away, and the lusts thereof, but whoever does Your will abides forever. And whoever urges something else speaks the devil's voice.

We don't want to be poor, Lord, as You know well. But help us decide right now that we'd rather be poor in earthly things than poor in things of heaven. And always be close beside us when the choices must be made.

Amen.

Forgiveness of Sin

If we say we have no sin, we deceive ourselves, and the truth is not in us. If we confess our sins, he is faithful and just, and will forgive our sins and cleanse us from all unrighteousness. If we say we have not sinned, we make him a liar, and his word is not in us (1 John 1:8-10, RSV).

Who stands in Your favor, Lord? Who deserves a seat of honor at Your right hand?

Not us. Not anyone we know. We all have sinned and come short of Your glory. None is righteous, no not one. You've told us this, and we know it, too.

Our sin pays wages, and the wage is death. Death not only of the flesh, but the soul and spirit, too. Death where there could have been life. Death that has no remedy.

Save us from that death, we pray. Don't let our sins take us down to ruin. Bring us, instead, to that cross on which our Savior died.

He was wounded for our transgressions—thank You, Lord! He was bruised for our iniquities—thank You, Jesus! He lived above, but died on earth, that we of earth might live above with Him.

We haven't honored Him as we ought. Help us do so now, we pray.

In His precious name.
Amen.

No Secrets Hid

Nothing is covered that will not be revealed, or hidden that will not be known. What I tell you in the dark, utter in the light; and what you hear whispered, proclaim upon the housetops (Matt. 10:26-27, RSV).

There are secrets we try to keep, Lord, even from You! How foolish we are, but we do it, we confess. Forgive us, and help us in seeking a more honest way to live.

What if all our thoughts about other people were laid bare and known to them, as they are to You? Wouldn't we have to do better?

What if the way we spend our money, every dime and dollar, was known so everyone could see it?

What if harsh words whispered in secret were brought out in the open and heard by all?

What if the darkest secrets of our lives were broadcast from the mountain tops? And all pretense should fail?

O God, from whom no word or deed was ever kept, not even for a moment—we'd need then exactly what we need now: Your saving grace and mercy on us all! For that we pray in our Savior's name.

Amen.

Steadfast Love

*I will sing of thy steadfast love, O Lord, for ever;
with my mouth I will proclaim thy faithfulness to all
generations. For thy steadfast love was established
for ever, thy faithfulness is firm as the heavens (Ps.
89:1-2, RSV).*

We've been afraid, Lord. Afraid for our health, and our
houses while we're gone. Afraid of strangers, and even some
people we call our friends. Afraid of storms, or steps we have
to climb. Afraid of what the future holds.

We're of little faith to let these things trouble us, of course.
And how they rob us of joy, and peace, and life's contentment.

Other times, we've had more confidence and strength. And
those were always the times of Your nearness.

Teach us, we pray, the lesson of trust. Let us see that earthly
hope is failing hope. But with You there's a steadfast love
which settles our lives on something sure and firm.

Do so more and more, we pray. And hear our prayer for
others who live in needless fear today, that they may know this
secret, too. Reveal to them Your love which casts out fear. In
our Savior's name, who often said "Fear not, I am with you."

Amen.

God of Our Salvation

Make me to know thy ways, O Lord; teach me thy paths. Lead me in the truth, and teach me, for thou art the God of my salvation; for thee I wait all the day long (Ps. 25:4-5, RSV).

You're above us, Lord, and beneath us, and all around us; before us, and after us. You sustain our lives daily, so each new breath is one more debt we owe.

You amaze us and confound us, walking in the mysteries of the universe about us.

You laugh at us, too. At how vain we are! At how we pretend to know so much!

And Lord, we know You cry over our many griefs. The things that hurt us hurt You as well. Especially when they seem to shut You out, as doors closed tight against Your love.

You break all rules we make to contain You. You frustrate all ambitions that take no account of You. You keep for Yourself all final words.

You ever love us. You heap Your mercy upon us. You forgive and renew us.

Beside You there is no other. We know it, and bless it, and kneel in surrender to it.

Amen.